HOW
TO
KNIT
A
HUMAN

ANNA JACOBSON is an award-winning writer and artist from Meanjin (Brisbane). Her poetry collection *Amnesia Findings* (UQP) won the 2018 Thomas Shapcott Poetry Prize. Anna's second illustrated poetry collection, *Anxious in a Sweet Store* was published with Upswell in 2023. She holds a Doctor of Philosophy in Creative Writing from the Queensland University of Technology. Anna won the 2020 Nillumbik Prize for Contemporary Writing and the 2018 Queensland Premier's Young Publishers and Writers Award. Her poetry chapbook *The Last Postman* (Vagabond Press, 2018) was published as part of the deciBel 3 series. She was a finalist in the Brisbane Portrait Prize, Blake Art Prize, Olive Cotton Award, and Marie Ellis OAM Prize for Drawing. Her website is www.annajacobson.com.au

How to Knit a Human is a precise and searching memoir that illuminates the fragile balance that can exist between memory and one's sense of self. The writing reflects superbly on the profound impact of memory loss caused by psychosis and its treatment, and shows us how storytelling can form part of healing through the sharing of experiences and a deeper understanding of them.

KÁRI GÍSLASON

In this wise, wry and moving memoir Anna Jacobson reclaims her self from the institutions that sought to define her. As she asks vital questions about care, memory and inheritance, Jacobson reminds us of the recuperative joy of creative life.

MIREILLE JUCHAU

This book is a revelation. If Leonora Carrington teamed up with Janet Frame you might get something close to the kind, gentle, weird and brutal brilliance of *How to Knit a Human*. Anna Jacobson has shifted my perspective on art and illness. 100 stars. Bravo!

KRIS KNEEN

How to Knit a Human is a visceral and immersive memoir, carefully crafted as well as genre-bending. Jacobson delves deep into her own unquiet mind only to emerge artistically victorious. A triumph.

LEE KOFMAN

Blazing, incantatory and furious, this is a work of unshakeable witness. Jacobson sorts through the shapes and shades of memory, dropped stitches and invisible repairs, to forge a blazing work of consolation and recuperation, a paean to resilience and creativity.

FELICITY PLUNKETT

In *How to Knit a Human*, Anna Jacobson gives us a sheaf of home made X-rays that net interior light. Her ability to stand both inside and outside of memory as an encased form has allowed Anna a rare set of insights, something akin to planting seeds in the air, that initially subsist then quietly grow under the moisture in her own breath. As writer, artist and musician, it is fortunate that Anna has the intellectual, emotional, familial and spiritual machinery to approach memory (as itself and herself), in a way that she can watch the pieces of the existential jigsaw move inside the box without her even touching them.

NATHAN SHEPHERDSON

HOW TO KNIT A HUMAN

A MEMOIR

ANNA JACOBSON

NEWSOUTH

UNSW Press acknowledges the Bedegal people, the Traditional Owners of the unceded territory on which the Randwick and Kensington campuses of UNSW are situated, and recognises their continuing connection to Country and culture. We pay our respects to Bedegal Elders past and present.

This book is the author's story and memory of events. Names and physical descriptions have been changed by the author where needed.

A NewSouth book

Published by
NewSouth Publishing
University of New South Wales Press Ltd
University of New South Wales
Sydney NSW 2052
AUSTRALIA
https://unsw.press/

© Anna Jacobson 2024
First published 2024

10 9 8 7 6 5 4 3 2 1

This book is copyright. Apart from any fair dealing for the purpose of private study, research, criticism or review, as permitted under the *Copyright Act*, no part of this book may be reproduced by any process without written permission. Inquiries should be addressed to the publisher.

A catalogue record for this book is available from the National Library of Australia

ISBN   9781761170041 (paperback)
           9781742238975 (ebook)
           9781742239934 (ePDF)

Internal design Josephine Pajor-Markus
Cover design Akiko Chan
Cover and internal illustrations Anna Jacobson

Contents

Cardea \ Stray stitch / 2011	1
Before \ The girl with the camera stitched to her side / 1992	5
Cardea \ Slip stitch / 2011	8
Before \ Stitching with sound / 1998	14
Cardea \ Free-motion stitching / 2011	17
Before \ Back stitch / 2003–2005	22
Cardea \ Memory stitch / 2011	27
Before \ Photo stitching / 2006	36
Cardea \ Conversation stitching / 2011	47
Before \ Stitching in stop-motion / 2009–2011	53
Before \ Pull / 2011	62
Before \ Night stitching / 2011	70
Cardea \ Glow-in-the-dark knitting needles / 2011–2012	86
Cardea \ A stitch in time saves nine / 2012–2013	96
Cardea \ Herringbone stitch / 2012	106
Cardea \ Zigzag stitch / 2012	113
After \ Owning your knitting / 2013–2016	126
After \ Social knitting / 2017–2019	143
After \ Trip stitch / 2019	160
After \ Unpick / 2020	165
After \ Unravel / 2020	179
After \ Patterns / 2020	192
After \ Woven overlay stitch / 2020–2023	200
Acknowledgements	209

To my mum, Sari.

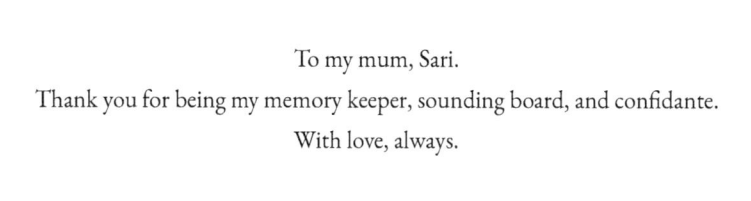

Thank you for being my memory keeper, sounding board, and confidante.

With love, always.

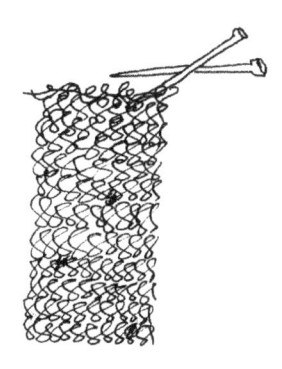

Remember the not-remembering. Knit through days and nights with words. Become a witch-wild surprise guest; a French-horn-wielding back-brace-wearer. Note their bulky shapes. Understand the making of your memoir is a ritual: join and piece your story together – try many times, in different selves, patterns. Experience postmemory, emailed miracles, spectral layers guiding the way. When the ghost light sings, do not take memory and sanity for granted. Do not take anything for granted. Collect your stray stitches while unhooking cicada shells that are never the insect itself, only the memory of it. Co-exist with the Goddess of the Door Hinge. Look through the comfort of the frame, or the wrong end of the telescope – all that's left of your face is an oval of white, no markings of self – obliterated memory like sun-washed film. Condense time. Change names and physical descriptions where needed. Discover the many forms help does and doesn't arrive in. An unintended vibrato translates an inventory: two balls of red string = truth, lies, a fabricated file, fire, trust, art, poetry. My story is my memory of events, released in my voice. Hold your breath, as your body is captured as an exhale.

And so, cast on.

Cardea \ Stray stitch / 2011

She finds herself in an empty white room with unmade beds. Driftwood washed up by the tide. Something momentous has happened. No one here to greet her at this important awakening. She feels as though she's been in a coma, contours worn smooth by sea. Something has happened to her memory. Taken and separated from her. When she tries to remember who she is – a slippage. Lying down, she recognises a hospital bracelet with her name. Anna. Nothing attaches itself to the letters. No memories of who she was or might be now. She knows her self from 'before' would be worried by this, but can only feel acceptance. And the sudden need to cleanse herself. She needs to wash away something invisible.

    To the left of her bed is an open door leading to a white-tiled floor and a shower. She undresses within the space. Turns on the tap. Realises she's forgotten to bring a cake of soap. A bottle of body wash awaits on the floor as though the container had known this might happen. She doesn't know who it belongs to, but the scent and colour is comforting. Orange. Surely the owner won't mind if she uses a bit. Held together by the smell of oranges, for a moment she feels like herself again. The scent cuts through the disinfectant she hadn't been aware of earlier. She turns off the tap. Naked. Looks for a towel and fresh change of clothes. Has forgotten to bring them into the bathroom. Wonders how she will get back to her bed without anyone seeing her. These things don't seem to bother her anymore.

There's a damp towel on the hook inside the shower door; she can't be sure it's hers. Its mouldy smell sours the sweet note of oranges. Instead, she puts her gown back on. It glues cold to her body. She needs clues. Answers. Her feet leave wet footprints down the corridor. She maps the space while she walks: a window embedded with pills set into a wall, and a large recreational room where a woman with curly hair greets her. A nurse. And yet the details jump together. Had she in fact walked down the corridor first on waking and did the nurse suggest a shower? Had she wrapped the towel around her rather than the gown? Or walked out naked to her bed to dress herself in her own clothes?

'Hello, Anna.'

The woman knows her name even though she doesn't know the nurse. Now is her chance.

'How long have I been here?'

The woman holds a clipboard but does not consult it.

'Six weeks. You've just had another round of ECT.'

She knows what ECT is. Electroconvulsive therapy. She feels like these words are the only thing she knows. She tries to keep hold of her expression. It is vital the nurse doesn't see she's upset. If the nurse knows she is upset, bad things will happen. She doesn't know how she knows this. All she wants to do is retreat to her bed, letting tears wet her face. She wants to know why the hospital has given her ECT without her permission but doesn't ask, as this too would be dangerous. Perhaps she has had this awakening many times before and forgotten, her self split over and over again. But this awakening is different from the others. She knows she will remember from this moment onwards, after a long time away from her body and mind.

'What month is it?' asks the woman, who has continued to watch her, as though observing the thoughts playing out across her face.

She considers carefully, knowing this is a test of some kind. April floats to the surface. She can see the word and its letters, the peak of the *A*, reflection of the *p* and lilting rise of the *ril*. If it had been April, as the month she seems to remember, then surely with whatever had happened, now would be the middle of May. The nurse writes down her answer and turns away, before thinking to correct her.

'It's August.'

Before \ The girl with the camera stitched to her side / 1992

Uncle Emil holds the video camera to his eye and walks in smooth movements like a dancer, capturing the family. I glance at the orangey-red M7 on the video camera's jet-black sides, but my eyes are all for the viewfinder and what it can see. The house is filled with my parents, my brother, cousins, aunts and uncles, great aunts, great uncles, Nana, and Grandad. I've spent the journey here watching for the bobbing full moon through the car window that often comes with Jewish festivals. The breaking of the fast for Yom Kippur tonight is no different. I am wearing my favourite dress – the one I just got for my fifth birthday with blue flowers and navy sash. As Uncle Emil films, I weave behind him through the members of my family like a cat. I want to know what he can see and what the world looks like through the lens. There is something distinctive about Uncle Emil. He is the recorder, the documenter. No one else films the family events. Something draws him to capture these moments that will soon become memories. When he pauses his filming outside on the balcony, I stare up at him, my need to look through the camera overcoming my shyness at the thought of asking.

'Please, Uncle Emil,' I say, pointing to the video camera. I want him to sense that I am like him – filled with a desire to capture and see the world as he does.

He looks at me then nods.

'Yes, for a short time, Anna.'

At the age of five, I do not know that Uncle Emil was born in Czechoslovakia and survived many of the concentration camps throughout Europe during the Holocaust. I do not know that beneath the long sleeve of his shirt, numbers from these death camps are tattooed onto his arm. I only know that his deep voice and soft accent is musical and specific to him, and that Uncle Emil never says anything about his past. He holds the camera up to my eye and I look through the lens. The lens is better than looking at the world with my own eyes, because I know I can keep what I see through this frame forever and ever.

He lets me press the record button and I capture the table on the balcony laden with Uncle Emil's famous homemade cheese, herring, pickles, olives. A rice dish with capsicum, egg, and celery. A pasta dish with walnuts. A tray of salmon patties piled high and teetering. From this low angle it looks like the patties touch the balcony awnings. Uncle Emil swivels the camera slowly to the right and I move my head with the camera. I see my older cousins sitting at the kids' table, laughing at the amount of food they have stacked onto their plates. They are too distracted to see I am looking through Uncle Emil's video camera. My parents don't realise I've had my first glimpse through a video camera either. Mum and Dad are busy taking care of my one-year-old brother,

Alan. My heart is flying at the same speed as film through a reel. This is a visceral feeling – one of joy.

At home the next afternoon, Mum waters the garden with a long green hose, while I stand on the grass. We have walked down the side pathway of our old Queenslander, past the macadamia nut tree and camellia plants with their heavy white flowers. I try to film the world through my eyes, but the comfort of the frame is missing. I open and close my eyes to mimic the video camera turning on and off, fading to black, but know I cannot ever play back a true recording. I walk across the grass and stand under the poinciana tree. Red flowers fall. If I had another set of eyes, I could look from the viewpoint of the verandah high above the poinciana tree at the same time and make a real film.

Sometimes I revisit photographs of myself as a child. I look at the photograph of me standing under the poinciana tree as closely as I can, to see whether the madness is there, hiding in my eyes, waiting to erupt. All I see is a girl who wants to capture the world through her eyes and art. There is no psychosis. There won't be for years. No forgetting that will split my self. The night I looked through Uncle Emil's video camera on Yom Kippur was the beginning. That night I would discover the world could exist as two ways of seeing. I could experience the world as it was happening, and I could also capture it for later. But I am yet to realise there is also a third way of seeing, and that to glimpse such a thing would take my memories from me, unravelling everything I knew, turning me into someone else.

Cardea \ Slip stitch / 2011

Would she ever have memories from the hinge of a person who wasn't her? August. Five months and a lifetime have been stolen from her memory. What happened to her body and mind while she was gone? Hinge. Unhinged. In Roman and Greek mythology, Cardea is the Goddess of the Door Hinge, a goddess of health who stops evil spirits from moving across thresholds. Her emblem is the hawthorn tree, which is thought to offer powers of protection. Later, when she discovers the goddess, she will like the idea of using her name for the hinge of her split selves. But she goes by Anna. Wants to be Anna. She is merely putting up with Cardea for now. She does not feel like she is back in her body yet. Someone else is still co-inhabiting her mind.

The nurse at the station is not as patient as the previous one who had told her it was August. This nurse gives her a 'wafer' and tells her to hurry up, but she can tell it's not a real wafer like the Arnott's kind with icing: strawberry, vanilla, chocolate. Her limbs feel slow as she puts the medicine in her mouth. It dissolves on her tongue like fairy floss. She drinks water from the paper cup to get rid of the bitter taste.

'You usually make a fuss. Had to give you the liquid form the other night. Changed your mind, have you?'

Surely this nurse can see she is not the same person she was before. She doesn't like the idea of her previous self being forced to drink a liquid. The nurse has upset her again.

'Don't mind that bitch,' says a woman in overalls, slugging back her water and binning the waxy paper cup.

The woman looks as though she is just on a pit stop here and is about to hop on a motorcycle and zoom away.

'I'm Joyce. You probably won't remember me after all your ECT, though. We're going to write a book together one day about our experiences.'

'I like your jacket.'

'Stole it from prison.'

She is glad to have a comrade in this place; glad there is someone other than the nurses who seems to know who she is. Joyce challenges her to a game on the broken pool table edged unevenly in green felt. They use their hands to roll the cue ball, marked with blue chalk. After, the meds make them both pace and together they walk from corridor to corridor.

The beds make and unmake themselves and the next day her parents and brother Alan are here. She is glad to see them and wants to give them something for their visit. She looks around, desperate to show some hospitality, and finally her eyes settle on the leftover Jatz and cheese sprinkling the laminate bench in packets. She is pleased she can offer them something to eat for morning tea. They take their findings out onto the barred balcony, and she introduces her family to her new friend, Joyce. She feels excited to know a woman so brave as to steal her jacket from prison. She wants her family to see how cool she is to have made a friend like Joyce. But Joyce says she is leaving today, and journeys away with the man in charge of her care.

One of the occupational therapists sets up a paper-marbling tray next to her, distracting her from Joyce's absence, along with the end of her family's visit. She once knew how to do marbling. Two girls are folding paper cranes in the day room – somehow, she knows they are trying to reach one thousand to make their wish. The girls see the marbling activity and join her, insisting that skewers are needed to swirl the ink to create patterns. But the OT says that pointy objects are not allowed; they'll have to be more inventive. Instead, she and Melanie and Katie pluck out strands of their own long hair to swirl the ink.

When it's her turn, she lays the piece of paper over the inky water, making a paper marbling pattern of greens and yellows. But when she lifts the paper, she sees she's managed to get an air bubble on it. The island in the middle of her marbling is like a breath. She feels connected to this anomaly on the page, more than the colourful headache of the green and yellow. Perhaps the air bubble's blankness is a small space of sanity that appears without beginning or end and resonates with her now. When the paper dries, she folds her marbling in half and puts it in her visual diary for safekeeping.

She plays Scrabble with a white-haired woman. They don't keep score. They make words like ANT and ECT, PILL and JATZ.

New patients arrive. One night, a boy is admitted into the women's ward. One of the girls tries to impress him by dancing on the pool table and falls and hits her head. The girl giggles while holding an ice pack.

The beds make themselves. She sits at the breakfast table. She loves the taste of the crunchy cornflakes with cold milk. She adds some sugar, and a nurse scolds her.

'You were meant to fast for your round of ECT this morning, Anna. Now we'll have to reschedule your treatment. How else will you get better?'

Get better. There is something wrong with her. She asks to call her mother from the nurses' station – cannot hold back the tears this time. She glimpses a photograph of herself paper-clipped to the manila folder of her file the nurse holds and is shocked by her appearance. In the photo she is not looking at the camera or wearing her glasses. Her hair is witch-wild, and her eyes are heavy-lidded with dark circles beneath. The nurse catches her looking. *This is you. Surprised?* The nurse's eyes mock her while her mother's words through the phone try to calm her. At dinnertime she lifts the lids on the plates of food sitting on the trolley. One is pork. She drops the lid swiftly and chooses another. It shines dark. Beef or lamb. She cannot remember if she has chosen the wrong one before this moment of awareness. At least tonight she knows what is kosher and what is not. The woman with white hair, and Melanie and Katie, push their desserts down the table to her to cheer her up. She has all the pre-packaged chocolate mousse, rice puddings, and strawberry milk she could ever want. The nurse with curly hair does not take the desserts away.

For lunch in hospital, they are served a treat – egg sandwiches on tri-coloured bread. She notes this in her visual diary. The beds make and unmake themselves. Time moves strangely in hospital. Sometimes it stretches like elastic with nothing to do. She's being wheeled down the corridor to have another round of ECT. She is scared she is going to die.

'I can walk.'

'This way will be quicker,' says the nurse pushing her.

They round a corner and enter a room. She is lying on a table. A team of doctors surrounds her. Even without her glasses, she can see they are all smiling at her. This is her last moment. She counts backwards from ten. Reaches five. Her veins turn cold, and a metallic taste fills her mouth. She regains consciousness as a nurse wheels her back up the corridor to the ward. She doesn't know how she got from the table to the wheelchair again. She notices a Milky Way bar in her lap, and anchors herself to the packet, looking at its stars and swirls – another awakening, though not as disorientating as the first. The Milky Way is her universe now. She craves plain crinkle-cut chips and Caramello Koalas. Like magic, her parents bring her a few packets of each. She devours everything while sitting alone on her hospital bed.

Before the beds can make themselves, a circle of blue-white cuts through the darkness like the light from a monstrous anglerfish. The light is attached to a male nurse, appearing at the end of her bed. The nurse holds the torch up to his face and grins, standing there for a full minute. He watches her, demon-like – so close she can see his stubble. She wishes he would go away, but he keeps watching her. He does not lower the light or move away for a long time.

In the morning she joins Melanie and Katie at the craft table again. She draws lines, shaky and light. Somehow, she knows she used to be able to draw but now can't. She presses harder into the paper but the lines are too thick. The OT praises her.

The drawings take minutes. She turns the pages to make more. In the next activity they make dream catchers, choosing long feathers dyed in purples and crimsons. She picks a special glass-blown bead to thread into the web. An amber one. Her fingers can't remember how to tie knots, so she loops the string until it tangles. The loose webbing could unravel at a single tug, nothing to stop the nightmares from flowing through the dream catcher's frame. But it holds together as though knitted by luck. She knows it should worry her that she can't tie the knots, but the strange feeling of acceptance again overrides the anxiety.

She wants to leave this place. She feels trapped and without time here. She wants to start writing and typing up her stories. Already she has circled some writing competitions listed in the back of an anthology. The anthology was printed in Melbourne. She will enter her writing in these competitions one day. She asks the nurses when she'll be able to go home or if there's a laptop she can use.

'Laptops are not accepted on the ward. After the doctor assesses you at your tribunal hearing you may be allowed to go on leave. Probably tomorrow.'

She doesn't know what a tribunal hearing is but recognises this precious word 'leave' that is whispered around the ward as though it's gold. Gold as the French horn waiting for her at home.

Before \ Stitching with sound / 1998

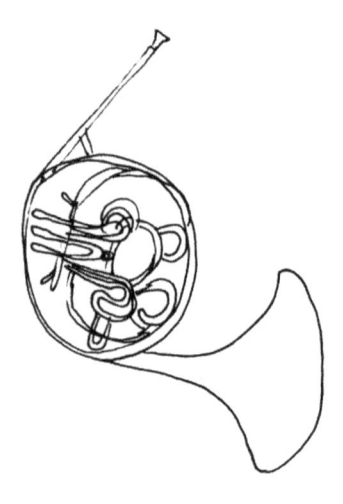

The music room looks and sounds like a fairground to my ten-year-old self. But instead of lining up for rides, I am lining up to try whatever brass, wind, or percussion instrument I like. At one end is the clarinet with its glinting black and silver intricacy. I queue up for it like I'm trying to get a prize from the claw crane machine. After each student tries to blow a note, the teacher takes out the reed and dips it into a cup of disinfectant. When my turn comes, I reach for the clarinet and lift it to my mouth. The reed tastes like chemicals; I can't get a sound out of it and am disappointed, like my turn has been rigged by the bitter disinfectant. Next is the flute that won't play a single note either. The instrument is removed from my clutches, and my turn is over. I feel like I've lunged with my mouth for the apple bobbing in water and missed. I begin to despair as I hear others around me get out squeaky shrieks from the clarinet and wisps of music from the flute. The music and sounds are their prizes. I can almost hear the *ding ding ding* of all their winnings. Maybe this sideshow alley of instruments isn't for me.

Then I notice a long line of kids in the middle of the room. I follow the parade with my eyes to the circus ring of excitement. Cradled in the teacher's arms is an instrument that reminds me of the giant golden goose egg from Jack and the Beanstalk. The instrument has three silvery keys, and one side-key for a thumb. I am transfixed by the maze of curled tubing, which ripples like two-layered rivers of gold. The instrument looks like it would make the sound of honeyed dew drops but no one can get a note out. This instrument does not have the sideshow alley vibe. It is the jewel of the show. Each student waits breathlessly to see if the next kid will be able to make a sound from it. Ignoring the drum-kit and trombones at the back of the room, I join the line for the curly-gold instrument, determined. Before I know it, I'm seated with the teacher and the instrument is in my lap.

The bell feels warm against my hand and when I spread out my fingers properly on the keys, I feel like I'm part of the instrument and the instrument is part of me. I place my lips against the mouthpiece, use air from the depths of my asthmatic lungs, and the instrument gives a muffled honk like a second voice. There's a gasp from the kids. I'm just as surprised as the teacher, who sits up straighter.

'That's a G,' he says. 'Try an F.'

I press down on the key the teacher tells me to use and make another muffled honk through the instrument. There's a cheer from the line of kids. A bell rings and time's up. The instruments are packed away, and I leave feeling upbeat, like I've managed to win something even though it was not what I was expecting. I'd wanted one of the prizes in the sideshow alley but had discovered a 3kg golden nugget in the dirt beneath the showgrounds instead. But still, there's no knowing which instrument they'd choose for me. Maybe the clarinet teacher would see my unfulfilled potential from across the room and pick me to play the clarinet.

I forget all about our auditions until I receive an envelope from the music teacher at school one week later. I open it in the lunch break. *Dear Anna, you have been selected to play the French horn. Please pick up your instrument on loan from the school office this afternoon.* At first, I can't remember what the French horn is. Did they mean a French clarinet? Then I remember the golden instrument that had seemed to come alive beneath my hands. I wonder what my parents will say when I turn up at home with a massive musical instrument.

I collect the French horn from the office. In its hard case, it looks like a shoe for a giant. I lug it to the turning circle, my arms aching by the time Mum arrives with the car for me and Alan. She helps me lift it into the boot.

'What on earth is that?' says Dad when we arrive home.

I open the French horn case and run my fingers over its soft blue velvet surrounding the coldness of the brass that warms to my fingertips when I touch it. The French horn seems to call to me, and I can see my face reflected against the bell, my eyelashes echoed in the tubing. I run a cleaning cloth over the brass to rub away any fingerprints. If I practise hard, then one day I know I could make its true bell-like sound. To care for the instrument, I follow the instructions in the *Standard of Excellence for French Horn*. I untwist the caps connected to the keys and squeeze three drops of oil into the rotors. I pull off the slides, one at a time so I don't mix them up. I grease the slides with a bit of red paste from a soft white tube. Who could resist this instrument? My parents look unsure.

'It's the same size as you are,' they say.

Cardea \ Free-motion stitching / 2011

Anna Jacobson   Surprise Guest

Alan gives her a gift: a miniature French horn in a black lacquered box, lined with red velvet. She keeps it in her bedroom at home for when she's allowed back again, not keen to have it stolen from the hospital. She wants to keep it safe. She is free – not completely free, but she is home with her family, on a leave day from the hospital. Her bedroom at home is hiding things from her. She spends hours going through her chest of drawers, rediscovering what she owns and where everything is. When she finishes looking, she forgets again. She opens her wardrobe and sees a monstrous pale pink metallic dress with puffy sleeves. She takes the dress off the rail and shows it to her mother. Perhaps a friend of Mum's was storing her clothes in her wardrobe while she was in hospital.

'What's this doing in my cupboard?'

'You bought that in Melbourne.'

'Really? Are you sure? It's not my style at all.'

She finds another dress she must have bought in Melbourne from the same shop, with a shape that doesn't fit her, and puts them both in the giveaway pile. There's a scar on her ring finger in the shape of a fishing hook. She looks at the scar's hook; wants to reel in its story from the ocean. The white line is deep enough to have sliced through her fingerprint. Now she is identifiable. She asks her mother if she knows the scar's story and Mum tells her of the flight for freedom: nurses and security guards chasing after her. The industrial security door had slammed on her finger. For once she is glad she has no memory – particularly of the pain.

Her woven bag hangs on the doorknob. Having a bag, phone, and her watch back again feels like a luxury. Mum gives her a care package, which includes a bag of liquorice, fluffy socks, some hair conditioner, and loose-leaf peppermint tea. The crooks of her arms are covered in pinpricks and bruises from blood tests. Dots twirl along her veins. At least a dozen in each arm. Blood-test confetti from a diagnosis party gone wild. She has a needle phobia. She's surprised by her own skin. Her legs are werewolf-ish and her monobrow has grown back. She plucks her eyebrows and shaves her legs furiously.

Mum and Dad take her to the Arboretum Park with Alan. The air feels fresh against her skin, and everything smells of the earth, away from the hospital. On the boardwalk, a black cat with yellow eyes suns itself and turtles poke their noses to the surface of the pond. She takes photos with her small digital camera. When her legs start aching, Mum and Dad drive her back home to get her overnight bag, and then on to the hospital.

'Wow, you had a makeover – your eyebrows. Where'd you get them done?' says Melanie on her return to the ward.

'I just did that myself.'

Melanie looks disbelieving. She gets the feeling that she must have been very unwell before this if Melanie thinks her incapable of plucking her own brows. She cannot be sure of time and its length. Her memory curls in and out in fragments. Dad appears around the corner, carrying a jumbo plastic bag filled with medications supplied from the hospital. Her time awareness pedals as if in response to her excitement – she's about to taste real freedom. Perhaps her prior leave day was a test she had passed. She walks with her father down the corridor for the last time. Melanie gives her several origami boxes made with patterned papers of zebra and crocodile skin.

A woman appears. She is too well-dressed and out-of-place to belong in the corridors of the public psychiatric hospital. The woman stands in front of her and Dad, blocking their path through the doorway like an annoying fly in a suit. She wants to push past her. Just wants to leave with her dad and go home.

'I'm your case manager. My name is Stephanie.'

Like two determined salmon swimming upstream against all forces, they continue to move through the door. She watches Stephanie frown and realises the woman does not understand the importance of her need to be free at this crucial point. She can't bear to stay here a second longer. Then she and Dad are out and into the car park and all thoughts of the woman who tried to waylay her disappear. She is free.

'Let's get something special from the Lebanese deli – any requests?'

Together they choose baba ghanoush and hummus with tabbouleh, baklava and Turkish delight. After lunch with her family, she sits on the floor of her room, trying to piece everything together. She takes stock: she is twenty-three and it is August 2011, one month before she turns twenty-four. She cannot remember her life. She unpacks her hospital bag and finds a visual diary containing a piece of paper marbling. More drawings from

OT activities, several plastic beaded necklaces, and folded origami cranes tumble out.

She turns on her computer. Displayed on the login screen is an extra profile user called 'surprise guest' with a picture of a blue macaw. She types passwords into the 'surprise guest' box but they won't work. At first, she thinks her family have been using her computer but somehow, she knows she created the profile. She is the surprise guest. Maybe if her memories return, or if she slips into the state that took her away in the first place, she'll be able to crack the code. Instead, she clicks on the profile user called 'Anna' and types up a diary entry in a file she's labelled *New Digital Diary 2011, Part 2*.

At night, she becomes convinced there's a murdering burglar upstairs in her family home, flattened against the narrow corridors, or folded into the linen cupboard. She knows it's an old fear from her childhood. There's no one there, but she can't be sure. Keeping all the lights on, she's aware that more infiltrators could be behind every closed door. But she does end up falling asleep, because the next day she can't remember what she's done the previous day. She feels like Drew Barrymore's character Lucy in the movie *50 First Dates*, without the dates. Again, the blue macaw profile pops up with the words 'surprise guest'. Still, she cannot get into its realm. She logs in again as 'Anna' and finds a file called *New Digital Diary 2011, Part 2*. She looks at the entry under the date. *Today I went for a walk and read my get-well cards.* The get-well cards she'd referred to are propped up for display. The messages from her friends are comforting and she can tell they do not know what is wrong with her, but that they are here for her whenever she needs them. She's glad she hasn't lost contact. The diary entry finishes with: *I replied to some emails and entered a photo competition.* She doesn't remember which photo competition she entered, but is relieved her camera is safe, waiting for her.

Before \ Back stitch / 2003–2005

For my sixteenth birthday, Mum and Dad give me my first digital camera that can fit in my palm. I cry knowing that I can now capture instantly what I see, as many times as I like until it's right. I can experiment with each photograph, without going through expensive film rolls or having to wait for them to develop. Alan hands me a purple fold-out photo album for all the photographs I will take. The camera becomes a permanent addition to my handbag along with my first mobile phone – a Nokia brick I was given the year before. Mum keeps all my drawings and photographs in an art folio, saying that I take after Nana. Nana is an artist – her paintings are as famous in my eyes as works by Chagall or Monet. As well as being an artist, she is the perfect nana – taking interest in what we are up to and finding us treats and gifts and kind words. I print my photos to take along to show Nana and Grandad. Every weekend my family visits the nursing home.

'Ellis, could you please get the grandchildren some chocolates – second drawer down under the books and in the black bag.'

Grandad passes us the box and we pluck out a chocolate each, carefully consulting the different types. Nana knows where everything is. She once told me she keeps a written draft of her memoir in a notebook in one of those drawers. I desperately want to read it. She is yet to type it out but tells me she started writing it when she was sixty. This was when her hands worked better before the multiple sclerosis worsened. There are photographs of Nana on the walls of the room from when she was younger. I look like her. I take digital photos of the originals of Nana as a young woman, so I have a copy to keep close.

'Anything special on this week, darling?'

'Just art class at school. We're each starting a new project and the teacher told us it needs to be inspired by an issue we feel strongly about.'

'That sounds marvellous.'

For the past year and a half, I have worn a back brace for scoliosis. Now I no longer need to wear it. On my last visit to the orthopaedist, he'd said I could even turn it into a giant pot plant holder if I wanted to. But I have other plans. The next day in art class I open my visual diary, embellishing tree branches with vertebrae so they form curving spines. I remember the making of the brace: a piece of plastic placed against my chest and then strips of plaster pulled tight around me – the plaster warm, but wrapped so tight I could barely breathe. Trying not to panic as lungs expanded against a hard cage. The brace maker leaned over me with a blade. He cut down on the plastic piece wedged underneath, the only object stopping the blade from going through me.

There are dozens of unusual materials that lurk in the art storeroom and by chance, two girls bring a heavy bucket filled with plaster strips onto our shared table. One soaks the strips in water and then moulds them together, so they harden into shapes – stars and moons. I sculpt twisted spines. Back in the art storeroom, there's a huge wooden board. Everyone else goes for the stretched canvases but the expanse of the wood works well for me. I just need to work out how I'll fix the brace to the board. Students aren't allowed access to the electric screwdriver, so my art teacher suggests I ask one of the design and technology teachers from the next room to screw my brace onto the board instead. The DT teacher doesn't ask what the brace is, but a few girls from the grade below me crowd around, watching. I want to hide the brace's exposed body that takes up so much space now that it's not around me.

'Hey, I have to wear one of them.'

I look at the girl who spoke, surprised.

'That's cool.'

I feel like I've achieved something through my artwork before I've even begun and creating the work now feels like the right thing to do. Once everyone has gone back to work, I pause for a moment, looking at the exposed brace, pale against the wood grain, and then begin.

I smear black and red paint over the brace with my hands. Something expressive is needed, not fine brushes. I remember all the hours spent pulling the straps at the back of the brace. The tight plastic against my stomach that made me feel claustrophobic in my own body. The angry welt across the lower left of my back that tingled. At night my ribcage had felt trapped against its will, struggling to expand. I cover the foam, plastic, and the sides of the board. Now that the awful blandness of the brace's original cream colour has disappeared, I feel it has become something else. A much cooler, edgier creature. I load the glue gun and let it heat up. Squeezing the trigger, the glue oozes and I run it along the plaster spines. The spines are like tree branches, writhing. I cover them in paint, blending them into the board so the spines seem to emerge from the inky well of the brace. Liberation. But something is missing. The room pulses: acrylic paint, glue, and the chalky smell of plaster beats through me, making my head pound. Stepping between palettes and stretched canvases, I head outside for air, not caring that the palms of my hands are still smeared with paint.

Outside the lost property office, I see a singlet and various items of clothing fluttering on the hills hoist for students to reclaim. I think of the singlets I had to wear every day under my brace and the Velcro marathon as I ripped at the bindings. My singlet would be damp from the heat of the day and peeling it off revealed red marks all over; the wrinkles and creases from the material mapped out over my skin. Standing under the shower was sensuous after having nothing but hard plastic around me.

The next day I bring in one of my singlets. I rip a hole in it. I retrieve a staple gun from the supply cupboard and press it against the singlet material and a section of the wooden board. Each staple is like a gunshot cracking through the air as I press the trigger. The singlet material now floats in the scene like a ghost. I fill the crevices with paint, creating and destroying simultaneously.

'What's that?'

I startle and see one of the girls from my class standing next to me.

'It's my old back brace for scoliosis.'

'Wow, I can't believe I didn't notice you wore one.'

I stand at the sink, paint running off my hands under the cool water and feel relieved now that it's out in the open. It's stuck on a board, and I am distanced from it. I have survived and now my artwork of my experience is complete. When I come back to sweep away the plaster debris, I see my teacher inspecting my work. For the past month I've had the painted brace facing towards the wall, only the attached backing of the wooden board visible. Now I wait for her critique, nervous. Her expression is unreadable and for a moment, misgivings stir. I try to reassure myself by knowing that the piece is honest and raw. I'm so tense I nearly don't hear her say, 'I'd like you to put it in the exhibition. I want your artist statement on my desk by Friday.' The end of term exhibition is only meant for the best students' work. From this moment on, I will create projects I am passionate about. This is where my voice can live.

Cardea \ Memory stitch / 2011

The memories she is aware of losing only appear with findings from files on her hard drive. To centre herself, she searches for digital photos of old art projects she's created – there's even an artwork with her painted back brace from high school. She also discovers she'd studied a subject called Photo History at uni. The essay topic she'd picked was to discuss Roland Barthes' description of photography as both an aid to memory and as eroding memory in relation to Susan Sontag's work.

As well as referencing Barthes and Sontag, she'd quoted photography theorist Geoffrey Batchen, who poses a series of questions to the reader, asking if they remember their childhood or only the photographs of their childhood. Geoffrey Batchen was right – photography had quietly replaced her memories with its own. But as her memories had been taken and replaced with nothing, the photographs were all she had.

She looks at old happy snaps she'd taken in the year before her 2011 hospitalisation. With some photographs, she can visualise the moment before and after the image was taken, like a hologram where she can see to the left and right but not beyond. But most remain a mystery, as though she's staring at a fake memory where her doppelganger is placed. No matter how hard she stares, some of the photographs just won't give way to the memory.

It's unclear to her how many of her memories have been forcibly taken. The split is not sharp and clean, like the one when she first awakened in a psychiatric hospital. This secondary tear is more nebulous and shifting, threads half torn before disappearing into nothing. She doesn't know the extent of what's missing because she can't remember. Can't gain traction. She needs prompting and clues to guide her. Only then can time begin to let through images and scenes to knit herself whole.

Her life in Melbourne in the months immediately before her hospitalisation remains a mystery to her. There's a file called Melbdiary.docx. Although typed, it seems hard to understand. The words don't bring memories and the sentences aren't complete – just snatches of phrases. She tugs at threads and manages to loosen one free. She reads: *Hands like ice, I haven't been able to eat or sleep for the last three nights.* She finds images from a photography job she must have been hired for at an old theatre space and scrolls through. She watches herself dance and paint with torchlight next to rusting stage lights. Whenever she is captured staring into the camera lens, she notes there is an intensity to her gaze. Looking back at the images of the theatre she realises she is a ghost in nearly all her self-portraits. She'd left the shutter open for long exposures, moving in and out of the frame, staying still just long enough to capture her outline. She makes these connections and keeps looking for the expression that may have been a clue to her incoming madness. Besides, it's only with hindsight that one can foreshadow. She watches herself blur. More clues. More mysteries.

She used to be able to eat books for breakfast, sail through their galaxies and be finished by lunchtime; disappear for hours. Now, she can barely dip her feet in. She chooses a book from the *Deltora Quest* series, one she has read so many times she'd practically known it by heart. But she gets stuck on the first page. Frustrated, she throws the book across the room where it thumps into the wall and lands awkwardly on its pages. She immediately smooths the pages back out.

Under her bed she finds a screaming face in thick black pen and a drawing of a woman whose eyes are fish. She throws the drawings in the bin, wanting no visual record from a time she can't remember, even though she usually likes to document and keep everything. She sorts through her emails again, replying to her friends, saying that she's been 'sick' but is better now. She spring-cleans her bedroom and cupboards, seeing and discovering everything all over again, hoping her short-term memory loss doesn't last. She asks her mother how she got the new scar on her finger and writes in her diary. Reading back over her diary, she sees she'd already recorded the answer several days ago – apparently, she'd nearly escaped the ward, chased by nurses and guards, only to have her finger slammed in the heavy security door.

Weekly psychiatric appointments at the hospital with an assigned psychiatrist are compulsory because she is still under an Involuntary Treatment Order. She packs her notebook and gets ready. Maybe this appointment will give her some clues. She sits in the waiting room with her parents for forty-five minutes. Anxiety gnaws the more she waits.

'Anna?'

She walks down the corridor to where the voice has called her name.

'Hello, I'm Dr James Scott. I spoke with you when you were in hospital.'

She shakes his hand; she is sure she would have recalled something about him had she met him before. His hair is red.

'I'm sorry, I don't remember you.'

'Don't you? That's okay; it was just after a round of ECT, so you probably won't remember due to the nature of the treatment. We had a long conversation, though.'

She focuses her gaze on the carpet near his shoe, wondering what she could have said to this man.

'You were very unwell. Your recovery so far is miraculous.'

'I want to know why it happened in the first place.'

'No one knows exactly why these things occur but it's all a mixture of timing, age, and genetics. We think you might have bipolar disorder. The Early Psychosis Team is here to research psychosis that happens in young people for the first time.'

Psychosis.

'Why can't I remember what happened to me?'

She wants to find out as much as she can. Her memories are missing, and she needs stories to weave herself back together. The gap in time and memory makes her feel split and not her self. She wants to know the reason why this happened and why she can't remember.

'The severity of the psychosis and ECT affected your memory.'

'If I don't write things down, sometimes the next day I'll have forgotten everything I've done.'

He shuffles his papers and brings out a form.

'There's a program called Mind Gym, which can help with your concentration and improve your memory. Due to the severity of your illness, you may never remember the time during your psychosis, but the program will help you in other areas. I'll book you in.'

Anything that would help her memory is vital and she hopes she can attend the program soon. She observes him write a note about Mind Gym, and she focuses on his watch.

An image – *a kind man sits on the end of her hospital bed. He is drawing something. A watch-face. 'Can you read the time?' the kind man asks. She looks at the long minute hand and the short hour hand. 'Yes,' she says and tells him the time. He looks pleased.* The image disappears. Perhaps this image was part of a memory of the psychiatrist in front of her; an image as she was drawn out of psychosis.

'Keep an eye on your mood. Usually after psychosis people become depressed,' he says as she leaves.

After the appointment, Dad tells her that Dr James Scott is famous for surviving lost in the Himalayas for forty-three days with nothing but two chocolate bars to sustain him. She will order a copy of *Lost in the Himalayas* and read how James was twenty-three when he was found; the same age she was when her madness hit. It was his will to survive, his sleeping bag, and hope that got him through. His sister wouldn't give up on finding him, even when all seemed lost. She reads that he also ate a caterpillar found in the ice and sucked on balls of snow for water. She feels a kinship with him that he has been through such an ordeal.

She is nervous about getting a haircut because of the state of her hair. At the appointment, she tries to rip through a matted clump with her hands so the hairdresser can comb through it. She doesn't want the hairdresser to know it's her first haircut out from the psychiatric ward. The side effects from the medications fill her with restlessness – her legs jiggle up and down under the hairdresser's cape. The hairdresser's bracelets jangle in annoyance as knots tear the teeth from fine combs. After this experience, she finds a new hairdresser and changes to a kinder and more accepting salon. A few days later, after she and Mum walk home from a visit to the café, they are surprised to see an irritated woman waiting outside their front door.

'I'm Anna's case manager, Stephanie. Your appointment was this morning. I was about to head home – no one was answering the door.'

'We weren't told there was an appointment here,' says Mum.

The woman slides a clipboard from her black briefcase. Her hair is cut in a severe line matching her mouth and she recognises her as the same woman who had stopped her in the corridor, after she'd been given the all-clear to leave the hospital.

'You were given ample notice. Can I come in?'

Mum unlocks the door. The woman sits with her back held away from the cushions on the couch in the lounge room, as though they are contaminated. It's Nana's couch – green-olive velvet, and very comfortable.

'I want to try some CBT with you, Anna. It will help with your residual anxiety from your episode.'

'What's CBT?'

'Cognitive behaviour therapy. We'll start with breathing exercises.'

The idea of breathing in front of this woman in calm measured breaths feels exposing and terrifying. Stephanie scowls when she says she doesn't want to do the exercises today.

'You want to be anxious forever, do you?'

She feels anger wash through her body and clench in her throat. How dare this woman, who already has so much power, come into her home and want to control her very breath. *You want to be anxious forever, do you?* She doesn't want to be anxious forever, but if she is, it will be through no fault of her own. She can sense Stephanie's disdain without looking and knows instinctively that a beast stands before her. She is devastated for the other involuntary patients who have this beast as their case manager. A static forcefield radiates from Stephanie – she can feel her case manager saying: *You need fixing / You disgust me / You will never get better / If I were in charge, I would tear out your throat / I hate you / You are a waste of time / You are nothing / I am more powerful than you.*

There is a beast in her home, camouflaged in a business suit, oozing poisonous words through her being. There is a beast in her home threatening her with her own anxiety. One day she will write back from this moment. She will hold the power.

She waits for James at the hospital. Today she's put on a beaded necklace and wears her favourite pair of pink jeans with her magenta owl top. Boys from the men's ward gather for a walk in the grounds. She doesn't remember ever being allowed to go for walks outside when she was an inpatient – she was probably too unwell.

'Nice necklace,' says one of the boys.

'Thanks.'

He has a fingernail with blue nail polish on it. On second glance she sees it's been scratched on with biro.

'Yeah, nice necklace,' says another.

The boys gather around her, complimenting her. James comes out and saves her from the boys' advances.

'How are you today, Anna?'

'I'm okay.'

'Stephanie said you didn't want to try CBT with her.'

She feels told-on and monitored. She wants James to be on her side. The last thing she needs is Stephanie whispering distorted lies to him. She wishes she didn't have to have the beast as a case manager. How can she explain to James that Stephanie had made CBT and breathing as appealing as chewing on a lump of tough meat rotting in the sun all week with farting flies and maggots?

'Her methods don't work for me.'

He makes some notes, his forehead creased. She doesn't want to waste the session talking about Stephanie and how awful she is. Fortunately, James changes the topic and asks her about her friendships. She tells him about her oldest friendship group, who had all written her get-well cards.

James nods and says, 'Those boys out there didn't bother you too much?'

'Nah, they're okay.'

He stops writing and looks her in the eyes.

'Sometimes after an episode of psychosis, people lose their warmth. But you still have yours.'

She smiles at the floor, trying not to cry. She is glad she still has her warmth, despite how her case manager makes her feel; glad she has someone like James on her side to tell her how she is or once was, with kindness. Sometimes she gets glimpses of memories from her favourite years – of being surrounded by the friendly students at art school, where her warmth had been welcomed. She misses her art school friends, scattered to the winds; they are now travelling the country and world, no doubt creating lifelong memories while she is rebuilding hers. She has lost touch with most of them because of her hospitalisation and wonders how they are now; she wants to get back in contact.

Before \ **Photo stitching** / 2006

At art school, I document my great-grandparents' passports from the treasure trove of the spare room, layering them in Photoshop with varying opacities, so that each layer peers through the other, obscured like memory itself. At night I suspend rocks tied to the towel railing in the bathroom and entwine my hair into the woven yarn scene. I take the photographs by torchlight, which has become my favourite way of lighting, using a laser remote to trigger the slow shutter speeds that trace my own movements.

Sharing my personal photography project, I am surprised when the class claps after my presentation. In the darkrooms, I get invited to my first uni party by one of the older students, who documents his life through the lens of his grandfather's Rollei twin-flex camera. When I arrive, the song 'Aquarius/Let the Sun Shine In' blares through speakers in the old Queenslander. Stacks of light-sensitive photo paper and rolls of film are packed in the freezer, bordered by icicles. The fridge is so full of beer, there's only room for one small packet of cheese. My photo friends pile out onto the back verandah. We sit on the floor and my back presses against the weatherboard. The talk is all about photography: where to get the cheapest film, digital versus film, and what type of photographer we want to become – art or photo-doc. I already see myself as an artist, capturing different realities of what is and isn't there. I get out my camera, using the flash with a slow shutter speed to capture my friends' outlines and movement traces. We discover more about each other's lives – some come from nursing backgrounds, others are social workers and mothers and musicians. They are excited to hear I also play the French horn. At the start of the year, I had auditioned to be part of the Queensland Wind Orchestra, wanting to keep up my French horn playing after I'd finished school.

I tell them how I take French horn lessons at the Conservatorium of Music. My teacher invites me to come to the brass warm-ups one morning a week and I am introduced to the other French horn students. I get a locker at the Con to store my instrument and then walk the ten minutes along the river at South Bank to the Queensland College of Art. I feel my photography-self and musician-self overlay, calling to each other and intertwining. It's like I lead a double life, but a life filled with purpose. I had passed my audition for the Queensland Wind Orchestra, and now rehearse every week in the Old Museum Building. The building holds a strange fascination for me. I head downstairs to the basement during rehearsal breaks, camera in hand, pushing past the old staff-admittance-only sign. Antique lace spider webs line the bannisters as I creep along. A single high-heeled shoe lies in a pool of fluoro light. It has lain there for the past year. Probably a misplaced drama prop from a rehearsal, I tell myself, trying to dispel the charged atmosphere. As my eyes adjust, I can just make out the crooked piano keys shoved under the staircase.

I document everything in my photographs so nothing can be lost. I don't leave objects and artefacts as they are but move the single high-heeled shoe and piano keys so they form circles around me. I bring them back to life. I paint with light, capturing a parallel of what I see lives within these spaces.

As well as being a member of the Queensland Wind Orchestra, I also rehearse with the Queensland Youth Orchestra II, where brass tutorials are held in the basement of the Old Museum Building. It's there I first find the old piano sitting among plumbing, hidden under the stairs, half of its keys scattered around the floor. I take an inventory of things I discover in the basement:

2	balls of red string
1	bicycle wheel
1	tangled washing line
5	storage containers filled with costumes
1	broken piano
16	snapped-off piano keys
1	scratched high-heeled shoe

Wind whistles through the exposed piano wires, sending eerie melodies around the room. A disused tap and sink stick out from a graffitied wall. I step closer to the piano, resting my hands on the gritty keys, my fingers pressing against the choked notes, only a couple ringing clear. All of them are out of tune but still awaken the space. I feel drawn to this room, this alcove of the building. I sense it holds possible mysteries, possible histories. The building bottles the music – lost cadences leak through pipes and drip between floorboards. Taking photographs in this space is like holding my breath, while my body is captured as an exhale.

I need to keep alive the piano's existence and story just as I often repeat my grandparents' over and over in my head so the threads don't become tangled and lost. Even catching my grandparents' details on paper is hard and ever shifting. Three of my grandparents each have their own tale of how they escaped to Australia, all part of the Jewish Diaspora. To me, the piano in this building represents these strands of tales – I can sense the piano's story woven into each of its scratches and markings.

I would never quite know the story of how the piano came to be in the basement of the Old Museum Building, just as I would never fully know the whole story of Dad's dad, who died before I was born. I remember my dad thought no one would be able to translate the lost document of my grandfather's story, written in a knitting of languages: Hebrew, Polish, and Yiddish. When Mum was pregnant with me and my grandfather was dying from bowel cancer, my great uncle had flown from Israel to Australia and transcribed my grandfather's words as he spoke. This accounted for the mixture of languages.

I remember learning about names and their origins in Grade four. I discover the name 'Anna' originates from the Hebrew form of Hannah, and my name is used in many countries and cultures: Italian, Czech, Swedish, German, Russian and more. I like the fact that my name can blend in anywhere. I give a presentation on where my last name comes from. I tell the class, 'And then the baker gave the Danish pastry to my grandfather and hidden inside was a passport. It was dangerous for the baker to help my grandfather, but he was kind. My grandfather ate around the pastry to get the passport out and that's how he escaped, and we got our last name Jacobson.' I pause and look around the classroom. Everyone seems quietly stunned, including the teacher.

'Thank you, Anna, for that interesting story,' the teacher says, and I sit down. I hope I'd done the story justice.

'Mum, do you know whatever happened to the man selling Danish pastries? Did he get into trouble?' I ask later.

'What's this about Danish pastries?'

'You know, in Dad's dad's story, how the baker hid the passport in the pastry.'

When she stops laughing, she says: 'No, no, Dad's dad just managed to get a fake Danish passport. Nothing to do with pastries.'

I am quite disappointed that pastries aren't involved. I had always wondered how he'd cleaned the custard and bits of melted icing from it. It seems my mind had embellished the word 'Danish', re-imagining the entire story.

I nag Dad about having his dad's story translated after I come back from another rehearsal at the Old Museum Building. I ask many times and finally Dad pulls out the script of my grandfather's story. We set about trying to locate a translator who speaks all of the woven languages. An Israeli professor suggests a Hebrew-speaking woman, whose grandparents happen to be Polish, who could help translate the document. We excitedly photocopy the pages and send her the file. I continue rehearsing in the Old Museum Building, and completing my photography studies, my mind wondering constantly about Dad's father's story and what we would discover.

Each of the photographs I take during this time in the Old Museum Building seems to hint at what I am trying to seek. Half a floral couch rests with the other side taken up by a ghostly presence, sitting on air. I capture myself in a self-portrait, peering into floor-to-ceiling cabinets as though trying to find answers. Every week I walk down the cobwebbed bannisters to visit the piano. Sound echoes around the alcove, before being sucked into the walls. Invisible fingers press down keys. I unpick harmonies, sew them into the velvet lining of my French horn case. Curved brass warms beneath my fingers. I rest my head against the piano's broken soundboard as though I am pressing a conch shell to my ear. I imagine vandals spray-painting basement walls and snapping off the piano's sharp keys. I imagine the pogroms of

Poland. I take handfuls of the loose keys from the floor. They smudge in my hands like charcoal. I return them to the piano one by one, and take out my camera to document the rooms. Past lives lie pushed to the edges: glass display cases, a peeling poster of sea turtles, faded pictures of hunting tools. Along the balcony, smashed-in aquariums fill with mouldy newspaper and weeds. Someone has written their name in the dust on the glass, and I realise the name is mine. The discovery is eerie. Someone else with my name haunts this space. I haunt this space.

I receive an email from Dad with the translated document attached. I print out the fourteen pages, looking at the paper filling the tray as though a miracle is taking place. So many small details suddenly revealed at once are overwhelming and the document shakes in my hands as I read the account. I follow the journey of my grandfather through the translated words. The story begins with my grandfather as a child: *Due to my age I couldn't go out to work, so I started to work at the black market. This is how we made a living until the war started.* Images of a secret movement spring into my head and I yearn to know more. What sorts of things did he have to do on the black market? The memoir doesn't say. Then the war started, and the Germans arrived close to their city.

My parents announced that they didn't want to leave everything behind again and run away. But they let the children do as they wished ... I decided to run away. The memoir doesn't mention what happened to his parents after their decision to stay behind. He formed part of the underground resistance. *In Zaltzburg we organised all the refugees and let them rest and organised as many families together as possible.* I wonder how many families they managed to save. The subject matter of my photographs begins to shift; I become a spectre on a staircase leading to an unknown destination. I create stop-motion works of shoes I find in cupboards, which walk themselves out of the scene to safety. And I capture sound. The echoing, ephemeral sounds of the building: of music, and murmurs through walls and cavities. The sounds of clues, diaspora, and leaving.

Many years later, Dad will read a sermon at our synagogue on his father's Yahrzeit, the anniversary of his passing. In his speech he says:

'After the war, my dad helped shift groups of Jews from Poland through the Czech Republic, to Vienna and then to Salzburg's displaced persons camps run by the Jewish Agency. He guided them over the Alps.'

My dad also speaks of what the memoir revealed.

'Dad was two weeks short of his 15th birthday when Germany invaded Poland on 1 September 1939. By fleeing Poland to Russia, he avoided being put in the Krakow Ghetto and likely death in a concentration camp. In Russia while still in his teens, he was drafted into the Russian army and served throughout the war in Stalingrad, Romania, Czechoslovakia and ultimately Germany. In difficult, often freezing conditions, he was somehow able to survive. He became an expert in explosives and defusing unexploded bombs.'

For me, my grandfather's memoir opens more questions and clues with no answers. Like being in the Old Museum Building, I must imagine its stories. As theorist Marianne Hirsch would describe it: postmemory. I want to discover what my grandfather felt. Want the kind of story that would let me connect to the person I had never known, who died just four months before my birth. The Old Museum Building can't tell me these things, as much as I try to find metaphors within its rooms. The account is important for its details about what my grandfather did and his amazing luck and skill in not getting caught. In one part, my grandfather steals wheat for his sister and her baby at night, without realising the grains are falling to the ground in darkness, creating a trace. My grandfather tries to cover the trace and cracks open the floor to hide the wheat. In another section, he must give his army commander his father's gold watch. Much later, after the war, he will escape prison by paying the demands of a drum of herring, six drums of vodka, soap, and half a million cigarettes. What I really want is the experience I have missed by not knowing him, and the questions I could have asked. But would my questions have been answered? Would the past have been too difficult for him to speak of, like so many survivors? In any case, he died before I was born and now, I want the impossible. My photographs continue to document the impossible in the form of moving light traces and stop-motion works where objects come to life in old buildings.

The Old Museum Building was once called the Exhibition Building. I find archives at the Brisbane Square Library with moth-wing-thin pages. Papery debris fills the cracked red spine. I choose another – this one with a navy cover, the next one brown. The oldest entry I find is from 1908. I read of the permanent water stains on the walls from flooding, and that once a rare sculpture was unearthed in the basement – no doubt put there for storage and forgotten about. I miss two buses while reading and don't realise it's closing time until a security guard clears his throat.

Lightning cracks an arpeggio across purple skies. The roads to the Old Museum Building steam with the smell of diesel on wet asphalt; petrichor. Droplets run along light fittings, fluoros flicker. Rivulets follow the same migration path, storm season after storm season. Plastic bins and buckets dot the studios like well-worn checkpoints on a treasure map, catching drop by drop. A red KEEP OUT sign leads to the loft. Rumours of storm damage and exposed electrical wires echo warnings in my mind. Another time, during a day rehearsal, I pull the latch, remembering hearing voices and footsteps from above as others explored. I climb the staircase and for a beat I glimpse an alien landscape. A white sheet flutters, stained with coloured light. In the centre of the arena is a white circus-like tent. And from somewhere, the sound of a vacuum cleaner.

In my third year of my photography course, I continue to document the Old Museum Building, my fingers flying over the camera on a shoot as I adjust settings with ease. With film I take time and move more slowly as each shot is precious. I measure light, capturing readings with a handheld light meter and spend hours in the photographic studios at uni practising using large-format 5x4 cameras. I stand with the black cloth over my head, hoping my calculations are correct. We learn different languages: swing and tilt. On my Yashica medium format camera, a roll of film will only take twelve shots in the shape of a perfect square. It's a different way of working. But the ground glass viewfinder makes the world look more beautiful.

I sit in the loft of the Old Museum Building, waiting for golden hour. I'd lugged my camera case in one hand and my French horn in the other, up two flights of stairs. Bundles of sheets lie at the foot of a vertical window in the loft. I slip off my shoes – the floorboards are hot from the setting sun. I set up my tripod and camera. In the loft, all sounds drift upwards, catching and collecting in different beats of space. I hear a cello song rising from one of the studios below. A haunting four-note melody, playing in stops-and-starts over and over. I decide on the best way to capture the space as dust motes drift. I adjust the camera and hear footsteps coming up the staircase. A boy appears, wearing all white, catching the last of the rays. He doesn't say anything to me as I stand with my camera and he disappears again down the stairs in bare feet, like an angel or a ghost. All is silent – the loft now cool-white. The magic energy has disappeared along with the golden light and the boy. The soles of my feet are black with dust.

I have since worked out the boy was from one of the community drama groups, who had come upstairs to adjust the sheet over the stained-glass window for the studio below, and its streaming afternoon light. But when I am deep in a photo shoot, everything is heightened and takes on poetry. I play back the scene on my camera, watching the space activate and myself dancing in stop-motion. I still think of the boy as an ethereal sprite of the Old Museum Building, wonder at the sight of him all in white. I am curious to know what he thought of the girl in black, camera stitched to her side.

Cardea \ Conversation stitching / 2011

She doesn't take as many candid photographs as she used to. Doesn't even carry her small camera in her bag anymore. This doesn't mean she isn't still observing and framing the world. She just doesn't want to record thousands of new moments yet; is still trying to reconstruct the old. Conversations are her new mode of documentation: interviews, almost. Her mother holds clues, but she doesn't know what questions to ask to unlock them. During this year, tea outings have started with Mum at their corner store café that looks out over the foothills and eucalypts of the Mount Coot-tha Forest. When the waitress arrives with her peppermint tea, she wraps her hands around the warmth of the china cup. The plastic sheets that stop the wind from blowing into the café distort the view of the Mount Coot-tha Forest foothills. She and Mum sit at the café for nearly an hour every day, and she still wants more. She is hungry for her mother's memories – how her mum saw the girls with anorexia brushing her matted hair and painting her nails fuchsia. Mum says she and Dad visited her every day and by the end of it, Mum knew the names of all the girls on her ward. Mum is patient in retelling her stories in answer to her questions – even though she's forgotten she's already asked the same questions days ago. Mum becomes her memory keeper, her sounding board and confidante. But the memories that should be hers only exist as versions in the heads of others.

After she walks back from the café, she checks her email. She's received a message that the list of finalists for a contemporary art prize, the Clayton Utz Art Award, is now online. Curious, she clicks on the link and sees a thumbnail of her photograph. She's one of the forty finalists. She reads the terms of the prize: her work will hang in the Clayton Utz offices on loan for a year and she will receive $100. And the chance of winning $10 000. When she checks the mail a week later, she sees an envelope addressed to her from the Lord Mayor's Photographic Awards. The words 'Congratulations you are a finalist!' beam out at her. It seems that all the good news is coming at once. Four days later, she checks her email and sees a message sent from an art journal saying that her work will be included in Issue Two. The only disconcerting thing about these emails and letters of congratulations is that she doesn't remember submitting to any of the competitions or journals.

She checks the dates of the saved photos on her hard drive and notes when their size was modified to fit the requirements for entry. She works out she must have sent in her photographs when she was on leave from hospital before her release. Her detective work pleases her. Maybe she can solve clues herself and find out her own story strands this way. She wants to be able to weave her memories together and not rely on others.

Two days later it is Rosh Hashanah, the Jewish New Year. Dad wears his suit, and she wears a patchwork sapphire, ruby, and emerald skirt with an embroidered black top. They drop off her photograph to the Lethbridge Gallery for the Clayton Utz Art Award before heading to synagogue. Walking along the side and back of the shul with its round stained-glass windows is like visiting a second home, a spiritual place for thinking. Before Dad walks through the doorway that leads to the men's section of the synagogue, he turns to her and says, 'We'll stay until after the sounding of the shofar and then I'll meet you out the front.'

Upstairs, she sits in her nana's and great grandmother's shul seat. There's nothing like the shofar sounding in the synagogue. It's the only time everyone stills and listens. The women stop their whispered catching-up with one another and the men stop shushing them. There's something ancient about the sound of the ram's horn and its call. When the rabbi plays the longest note at the end, *tekiah gedolah*, his face turns red with the effort of trying to make it last for as long as possible. The note goes on and on, wavering and then getting stronger until finally the rabbi runs out of breath. 'Shkoyach!' the members of the congregation exclaim – the rabbi has done a good job.

When they get home, she brings out her own shofar. She still remembers sifting through the cardboard box filled with ram's horns at a Judaica shop. Despite her French horn playing, she couldn't get a proper sound. But when she found the curved black shofar that looked like polished marble, her sound was clear and clean – just as she imagined it would be. Despite still feeling torn into two selves, she is glad she could hear the shofar in shul and knows it can only bode well. At her aunt's and uncle's house they wish each other *Shana Tova* and toast to a happy, healthy, and sweet New Year. She's made Nana's honey cake recipe, and when left in the fridge overnight, the top goes sticky like hers once did. They serve it with dark chocolate, berries, and gelati.

When the day of the finalists' morning tea for the Lord Mayor's Photography Awards arrives two weeks later, Dad asks her if she wants to go, knowing she is still recovering. She says yes. When they arrive at King George Square, right in the centre are a series of foldout chairs and a microphone. The photographs are unveiled; they've been printed over a metre wide onto weatherproof canvas, flying above the space. Hers is a photograph of her hand holding a suitcase made from squares of film, and across the squares are postcards and envelopes addressed to her maternal great grandparents, flowing with stamps and her great grandparents' Ketubah – their Jewish marriage certificate written in Hebrew. She'd named the photograph 'The Letters' from her series '59 Clues and a Bag of Bobby Pins'.

The work is an extension of the Diaspora photography series that she'd created in her first year of art college in her photography degree. In her Diaspora series she'd layered together photographs, passports, and old diary entries. She'd found fabric to tear through, assembled rocks hanging from string, and even woven her hair into the string so that it curled suspended from the room. In the last image, her photographs from the series are stitched together to find meaning. She'd finally found a visual way to communicate this search, through layering, assemblage, and piecing together. Since then, her photo series have echoed these motifs.

They sit in anticipation in the beating sun, as the announcements begin for the Lord Mayor's Photography Awards. Both her parents, while trying to look upbeat about her release from hospital, have appeared haggard to her, with dark circles beneath their eyes and strained expressions. Now she sits next to Dad, waiting as the MC walks to the microphone to announce the open category. Winning would be a wonderful surprise after everything that has happened. She daydreams in the pause of breath before the winner's name is announced. Maybe, her mind skips ahead of her, she could even afford an upgraded camera. Her current Canon 350D, which saw her through uni, had 8 megapixels, and she's been researching the Canon 5D Mark 2 series that has a whopping 21 megapixels in comparison. The resolution and level of detail would be impeccable. But the announcer's mouth opens and closes, and her name isn't called.

'Never mind, let's get out of this sun,' says Dad, whose words try to mask his disappointment for her.

But before they can quietly disappear, they're whisked into a room for the morning tea. There is apple and guava juice, cucumber sandwiches, a fruit platter, mini passionfruit meringues, and all the chocolate fudge diamonds she can eat. She has one of everything, her meds increasing her appetite by the second.

The Clayton Utz Art Award night arrives, and she can only take one guest, so she goes with Mum this time. They arrive early and take the lifts through the spangled-lit building along Eagle Street Pier. Lights flicker like fireflies far below and weaving their way through the rooms is like a treasure hunt to find her artwork. The photograph she'd entered this time is a self-portrait. In the photograph she's travelling in a rocking chair through the air with a yellow parasol, flying high above rock pools that look like cooled lava. She's also wearing a red dress that her nana once wore when she was younger.

'It looks amazing, Anna. Congratulations,' says Mum, giving her a hug.

They walk back into the main area where there are canapés and drinks and laughter. She hears her name called and recognises her friend Heidi from her photography school days.

'Anna! I haven't seen you in ages! How have you been?'

She feels happy to see Heidi, but also secretly panicked, not wanting to be caught out with her memory. She is still on the waiting list for the Mind Gym program. Having simply recognised her friend after psychosis and ECT is an achievement for her.

'I've been okay.'

'Which artwork is yours? Show me,' says Heidi.

They make their way back to her artwork. Mum is enjoying herself and it's hard not to get caught up in the excitement. When they are ushered into a room for speeches, she wants her name announced as the winner, but doesn't want all eyes to turn to her. The flash of cameras, the surprise meeting of her friend, and the possibility again of winning $10 000 makes her feel nauseous. Mum squeezes her hand in the breath before the winner is announced, but again her name isn't called. Heidi invites her to party on with the winning artist and go out for drinks, but she knows she can't. Already she has used up all her energy reserves. She makes her excuses and travels back to the safety of home with Mum. But she knows her photography will continue to get her out into the world, as it has always done. Even if she isn't taking as many photos as she used to, there are still old buildings to explore and people to preserve on film. She needs art to both express herself and engage in the world this way. Otherwise, perhaps she would never go outside or see anyone at all.

Before \ Stitching in stop-motion / 2009–2011

The Photography Honours program doesn't have as many shared subjects with other students, and is more research-driven – a solitary and isolating experience compared to the first three years of uni, when I was surrounded by my art friends. I begin to feel that something inside me is derailing and losing its way, as though the train I have been on has torn itself from the tracks and ended up in darkness. I cannot see clearly through my glasses. I tear through every eyewear store in Brisbane, trying to get the right prescription and leaving a trail of lenses and frames behind me. My blurred vision seems to herald much more than worry over whether my photographs are sharp or not. I show Mum my latest pair of purple glasses that I've been trying to convince myself I can see out of.

'The optometrist said they really suited my personality.'

I was unsure of them at first, but when I told the stylist I went to art school, he said they would make a good statement. He explained that even though I seemed quiet, they expressed my true nature. I didn't know how a stylist who barely knew me could sense anything in five minutes, but the frames were my favourite colour, so I bought them. I can tell Mum is being as careful and tactful as she can.

'I think they're a bit too big for your face, Anna.'

When I turn up at art college, my art theory supervisor shows me the corrections to my exegesis, which I have titled *Imagined Narratives: Cultural Identity and Memory in Photography's 'Third Space'*. But her markings are a blur.

'Sorry, I can't see, I'm still getting used to my glasses,' I say.

'Yes, I think I'll need to get used to them too.'

I'm taken aback. Surely my glasses can't be as wild as all the coloured mohawks, tattoos, and crocheted dreadlocks with hair-jewellery I've seen on campus.

Mum accompanies me to my next optometrist appointment for moral support. She can't understand why my prescription can't be sorted. After another couple of attempts with blurry lenses, and after another highly recommended optometrist tries to take several readings, he suggests I take up yoga.

'You're not relaxed enough. It's too difficult to take a proper reading. And where did you get those frames? The width of them is probably distorting your peripheral vision.'

Mum suggests I see an ophthalmologist instead. But I am so distressed at the thought that the specialist cannot get my prescription right, I burst into tears each time she brings the letter chart near me. Finally, the ophthalmologist suggests I sort out my mental health and asks me to come back when I am more relaxed. She tells me I am so stressed my vision is being affected, which is why the optometrists can't take an accurate reading.

I figure the stress affecting my eyes is just a blip. Everyone gets stressed in their Honours year, but no one else I know has told me they are seeing shrinks. When I take off my new glasses to swap with my old pair, I see violet frames with lilac zigzag stripes arching diagonally downwards like frowning eyebrows. The sides are as wide as purple goggles for a science experiment gone wrong. I don't know how I could have been talked into choosing such a pair of frames. Maybe a shrink could help after all. But I can't make myself take the giant leap, so I decide to start off small and seek help from a recommended counsellor instead. I book in and when my appointment arrives, I sit in the tiny waiting room next to the water cooler. I'm on my second cup of water when the door opens, and I am ushered into a room. I am nervous, wondering what questions the counsellor will ask.

'Why are you here?' he says.

I instantly tear up. How do I explain the intense stress, anxiety and dread I feel?

'In my profession I'm not allowed to give hugs to comfort a person so instead I do this—' and the counsellor leans forward and vigorously moves his hands across both of my kneecaps. I'm so surprised I just stare at him. I hadn't heard of the rule where the touching of knees was allowed.

'Now, I want you to swear,' he says.

'I don't feel like it.'

'It's important you get out your anger.'

'I'm not angry. I'm confused.'

'Swearing will help.'

'I'm not a swearer.'

'Just swear to show me how shit you feel.'

I can feel my blood pounding and am frustrated that I will not receive the help I need.

'Stop playing games with me.'

'I am most certainly not playing games with you. I can see you're in no mood to cooperate. I'm going to have to ask you to leave for today.'

'But I need your help.'

Surely there is some piece of wisdom he can say to help me.

'I think it's best you leave now.'

I escape and sit in the sun in King Edward Park, near bustling Central Station. I can't make sense of the counsellor. Seeking help has only made me feel worse.

I throw myself into stop-motion photography and combine this with my writing and poetry. I experiment with video-poems by smudging words with tea and ripping through the paper in a stop-motion sequence. One evening at dusk, I sit on a rocky step covered in vines and in the last of the sun's rays, I capture my hands' shadows. I discover a rusty chandelier hiding in the garage, probably from my great grandmother's time, and bring it out. I shine a torch over it, capturing the light's movements. Using food dye, I create a blue wash over my line drawings and words, as though they are engulfed by the sea. I create footage of drawers opening and closing themselves; handles and locks turning. When I play the images together, the words dance. I decide to go to poetry readings because I have been writing more. I have started scribbling fragments of my words onto pieces of paper, the backs of bus tickets, scraps of envelopes, and anything I can find.

I toss myself out of the house with a poem I've written in the process of making my video-poems. I catch the CityCat and sit at the back, looking at the wake of the vessel cutting through the river, feeling the slight rocking of the waves as other speedboats echo past. When we pass under the Story Bridge, arching its way high above, I know New Farm is not too far away. I then follow the map I've drawn from Google to help me remember the way, walking through the rose gardens to the basement of the darkened Alibi room where SpeedPoets is held. I step my way through the poets and sit on a spare cushion on the floor, knee to knee with everyone. Some sit on milk crates. A guitarist improvises tunes as the poets read, creating a whole new level of atmospheric performance. Only a few lights glow in the darkness, and I feel like I've stumbled into an underground cave filled with poets and their spells.

I can't bring myself to perform the poem I have scrunched up on a piece of paper in my pocket. My anxiety has begun to tumble out of control, so getting out of the house and coming to a new place by myself has been hard enough. I listen as different poets read their poems. I've diverted into an alternate universe where my language is spoken. Half-way through the readings, tears run down my face. I don't know if I am crying because I am so connected to the poems, or because I am sad. I don't want to bring attention to myself and hope no one can see me in the dim light. But I catch a kind-looking woman glancing my way. After the performances, she asks me what brought me here. I know I must look the youngest out of everyone. 'I'm a poet,' I want to say, but instead I mumble something about Googling poetry events. I disappear before more questions are asked and make my way back to the big blue and yellow CityCat, passing the Moreton Bay Fig trees lining the hill above the river. When I board the CityCat I stand at the bow this time, letting the wind whip away my thoughts. I breathe in the scent of the river. The CityCat takes me all the way back to South Bank where the bougainvillea blooms bright fuchsia and orange.

I now work two casual jobs: one at the art gallery as an activity assistant, where I spend my days sharpening coloured pencils and handing out bright stickers to children. By night I work as a theatre usher, where I tear hundreds of tickets in under fifteen minutes and catch glimpses of shows and plays from the sidelines. I want to write my own play and am inspired by what I see. But the most I feel at peace and fulfilled during this time is sitting next to Nana, who is typing up her memoir. The nursing home has recently bought a computer for the residents to use. I remember how I have wanted to read Nana's handwritten draft since high school and now here I am, helping navigate the computer so Nana can type and save her work onto the floppy disk. Nana's fingers are in the correct position, typing with slow, perfect precision, except for her pointer and ring fingers, which have seized up from multiple sclerosis. Next time I visit, Nana's hands are clawed and don't press well, so I offer to type. Nana rattles off brilliant-sounding paragraphs, intimate details of her life. My fingers skate to capture the magic of her words. I don't want to tell her to stop, so I push myself to catch each phrase, each story. Nana's musical dictation plunges me into the scene.

At school her friends called her the Polish princess. Now Nana is a regal queen, and I am her loyal subject. Her memory is sparking and the keyboard electric with her tale – last week it was escaping the pogroms in Poland. This week is the final paragraph. She writes the 'Shema', a parting prayer. There's a feeling of completion, her legacy captured by the two of us. I hug Nana through the arms of the wheelchair, sink into her soft skin, breathe in her scent. How to describe Nana's scent? It's made from the allspice of one hundred honey cakes. Of talc and perfume. I also sense scents from her previous homes: cedar mothballs and salmon patties; the aniseed from a pantry filled with black jellybeans for grandchildren. I wheel her back to her nursing home room where Grandad is resting. Nana's paintings dance the walls in oils and charcoals, abstracts in watercolours and Indian ink. Carved candlesticks illuminate a Shabbat dinner, fire becomes spirit.

One night, Dad answers the phone and tells us that Nana has suddenly passed away. There had been no warning; we had visited Nana and Grandad at the nursing home only the other day. It is night-time and all the lights are on. No one can be comforted. The corridor shadows turn the stairwell into a moving beast. Jewish funerals are held within a matter of days after the death of a loved one. After the funeral, instead of driving Grandad straight back to the nursing home, we take him to our house. He eats some homemade pumpkin soup and asks again: 'Where's Adele?' His memory has hitched a ride with her soul. His story is so entwined with hers that he is lost without her prompts of where things are, what they're doing today, who he is. Mum unlaces his shoes, and he lies on the couch. I watch over him, his vulnerability visible.

'Where's Adele?' he asks, and I tell him, softly, that the funeral was today, explaining to him that he went. I watch him realise all over again that she's gone.

On a rainy day I scan Nana's photo negatives I find in an envelope in the study. All it seems I can do is sit and scan, while the light flickers. I discover more amber strips of film containing images that had not existed in my memory-collection before. Some of the images I recognise from scrapbooks and albums, but when scanned straight from the negatives, the colours are now brighter and are no longer faded on the paper. More of the image is revealed from the scans I make, beyond the edges cropped off by the border of the print from the labs. I now have an extra centimetre of the images: the end of a branch on a tree is revealed along with three other people. I pore over the details. I decide photo restoration could be a career option for me. Maybe I could find a job like that. I do an online search and include the word 'photography'. A job description appears: not photo restoration but a photography opportunity for the Melbourne Zoo. I put together my application and send it in, hoping my Honours degree in photography will give me a better chance.

I feel the need to disappear from Brisbane and find out what life is like surrounded by more of my culture. At work the next day during the matinee shift, I watch the river flooding its way towards the Cultural Centre. I sneak glances through the high-ceilinged windows of the theatre foyer for the rest of my shift, hoping I can get home. After the show ends, I attempt to catch the train home from the South Brisbane station in the rain. The carriage is full of workers who have been sent home early, not knowing if they'll be able to make it back. I change connections at Roma Street. But as rain lashes at the windows, there's an announcement that Indooroopilly is flooding, and the train can't make it to my stop. I get off a stop earlier at Taringa, and ring Dad. He picks me up within ten minutes and drives the back roads that haven't yet flooded. It's upsetting seeing familiar places underwater and destroyed on the news, people clambering into tinnies. Our home doesn't go underwater but the muddy destruction around me feels like another sign and push for me to leave this city. Every time it rains, I feel uneasy. Perhaps I should have known that with the January Brisbane floods, 2011 was up to no good.

My Melbourne Zoo photography application has passed to the next round, and I'm invited to take part in an interview. It's time to stop searching from afar and try my luck for a job in-person in the city. Even if I don't get the job at the zoo, perhaps I could find a job more easily by walking the Melbourne streets on foot. I search for a place to stay in the biggest Jewish suburb in Australia – Caulfield. It's April, and Melbourne is calling.

Before \ Pull / 2011

I arrive in Melbourne, my purple suitcase laden with Passover macaroons and fruitcake in snap-lock packets. I walk along Kooyong and Glen Huntly Road, taking photographs of all the Jewish stores and signs. At Coles there is a large kosher section. I catch a train to Balaclava. An old man holds up his pants, at least four sizes too big for him, his cracked shoes dragging from his swollen pancake feet. I am shocked to see he wears a yarmulke and I wonder about his story. I have never seen a homeless-looking Jewish person before. He shuffles along the train platform.

Along Carlisle Street is a sushi shop, selling kosher sushi on Tuesdays, Sundays, Thursdays, and Fridays. I catch the train and find myself back at Glen Huntly Road. I buy an onion bagel at Glick's for $1. In the warm bakery, kids in yarmulkes choose cupcakes next to a display of blintzes. A group of elderly women and a man order Devonshire tea with bagels instead of scones and tall mugs of coffee. I have never experienced this level of inclusion before; never experienced so much recognition of my culture in the form of baked goods, a bookshop dedicated to Judaica, and an art gallery representing Jewish artists.

I've been told to bring my camera for my interview at Melbourne Zoo. The following morning, I lug the SLR on the train to get to the zoo at Royal Park Station. On arriving, the interviewers give the group of sixteen eager photographers the brief for the photo session: we are to capture three animal portraits; two of these photographs need to include visitors, and one image must represent the face of the zoo. It's the most unusual interview I've ever participated in.

'You have forty-five minutes!'

The photographers scatter, sprinting around the zoo, trying to find the most interesting animals to photograph. Because I'm new to the area, all I can find at first are the restaurants with screaming children dripping their ice creams onto fake plastic animals. I move further along and wind up at the ostrich enclosure. Their necks are so long I can't get the whole animal in the frame and end up just focusing on their heads. They stare back at me dolefully – perhaps not the best image for the 'face of the zoo'. I decide it's best to move on.

I enter a darkened plastic cave and find myself among the snakes and amphibians. The glass enclosures are reflective and the lighting too dim to get a good shot here. I try not to panic as I zigzag through the zoo, feeling as though I've missed the race entirely. It's now the middle of the day, so the lighting is harsh and terrible to work with. Fortunately, feeding time has begun for the giraffes. I take a close-up of one giraffe's long purple tongue winding around the food. I find myself lost again and the photographers in my interview group run past wearing frenzied grimaces of support.

'Zebras are to your left!' one shouts.

After, I head to the photo station to choose my best images, but time is nearly up and there is no time for sorting. As a penalty, I must hand over my memory card, with the good shots interspersed with all the outtakes. After fifteen minutes the woman calls the group together and splits us into two. My face still feels red and sweaty from the run around the zoo. I look at the division, seeing that there must also have been a category for interviewees who look like they've just breezed out of a modelling session. I know what is coming. The instructor turns to my group on the right.

'Thank you for coming, unfortunately your group won't be continuing with the interview. Feel free to enjoy the zoo before you leave.'

Trying not to feel too downhearted, for our free day at the zoo, a few of us decide to explore and take more photos despite the rejection. Once the pressure of the interview is off, the shots come easily. We discover a seal enclosure with light streaming down in rays through the ceiling-to-floor glass tank. I take several photographs and the result is magical, the seal breaking through the surface of the water in a deep dive. I won't give up. I know I can still make it as a photographer. I've always loved memory and photography and decide to apply to be a digital photo-restoration assistant.

That night, I type in the key words 'photo restoration' and 'Melbourne' online and discover a studio a few suburbs away. The next day, I catch the train and walk a couple of blocks to the address. The icy wind bites through my clothes on my journey.

When I find the right number – an ordinary house and not the studio I was expecting – I summon the courage to knock on the door. The man who answers seems surprised to see someone who has come all the way to his house to hand him a resume. He says he's been thinking about getting an assistant for a while and asks if I want to restore a photograph as an on-the-spot interview. I say yes.

He makes me a cup of tea, first turning on a spare computer for me. I look at the image he's loaded onto the screen: an old photograph of a young soldier, possibly from World War One. Deep cracks run through the photograph – the left side of the soldier's face has faded away, including his eye. I sit down to reconstruct the image, tea untouched. I feel like I'm preserving the past, building with pixels to capture old ancestors. I mask the crack running through the photo, as though it has never been torn. One part of me loves the marks and creases that age brings, and I want to build my own digital catalogue of these textures. Another part of me knows that the owner of the photograph wants the image returned as new as the day it was created. I'm not sure how to tackle the soldier's left eye with the pixels available and start work by copying and flipping the pixels from his right eye. The reconstruction of the soldier's features is tricky and after twenty minutes, I stare back in horror. I barely have time to get rid of the third eye that has inexplicably appeared before the man looks over my shoulder at my progress.

'Ah yes. Well, I did give you a hard one, never mind.'

I leave the house to make my journey home and he says he'll be in touch, waving from the door.

Dad is flying from Brisbane to Melbourne for a conference. He asks if there's anything I need that he can bring. I ask for my graphics tablet and hair dryer. The graphics tablet will be useful for my photo restoration work, and make the refined Photoshopping easier, even though I am more comfortable using a mouse. That night, I go for a walk with Dad, showing him all the Jewish signs of Glen Huntly Road, despite the shops being closed for the day. We head to a nearby restaurant that is warm and friendly, and smells of frying garlic. He is pleased I seem to be settling in. I order the mushroom gnocchi. He gets the Moroccan fish and tells me to *eat, eat*. I tell him about trying to find a job, the disastrous zoo interview, and my attempts at photo restoration. He says not to get too dispirited, that something will turn up.

But one week passes without word from the man at the photo restoration studio. I decide to build up my courage and call to see when he would like me to start. He sounds distant and apologetic on the end of the line and explains he doesn't have as much work as he thought. I know I have not passed the interview. Not dissuaded, I print another batch of resumes at the printing shop down the road and visit a second photo restoration studio. When I hand in my CV, the owner says he'll call me, but I get the feeling he'll say no too. I ask him for a trial, and he reluctantly says yes. I navigate my way up the creaky wooden staircase to the studio above the shop. This time, when I work away on an old family photograph, I feel like I've done a good job. I colour adjust the image, add more contrast so the picture doesn't look as faded, and clone out the cracks in the foliage behind the smiling faces of the family. The challenge is easy compared to the work that had been required for the soldier photograph.

The owner says he'll inspect the image and let me know the outcome later that afternoon. On my way home, I pick up a one-kilogram pumpkin and two cloves of garlic for $3. I am pleased with my thriftiness and decide to make a batch of pumpkin soup for my lunch and dinner for the next three days. When

I get home, I cut up the pumpkin and let it cook on the stove with boiling water and a stock cube from the pantry. The soup on a low simmer, I head upstairs to check my email. I've already received a reply from the studio: *At this time you are far too slow with your Photoshop and to expect a payment of $20 per hour for your current ability I feel is excessive, I would not even consider $10.* In 2011, ten dollars is well below the minimum wage. The insult sits heavy on my shoulders. When I check the soup again it's burnt; the base of the pot blackened. I blitz the mess and then scoop the mush into a Tupperware container, determined to still eat it. But I can't stomach it yet. Instead, I make ginger tea in the freezing kitchen and rethink my next move.

Melbourne has over twenty theatres, so I send off emails and resumes to every theatre I can find. I write in my cover letter that I have a photography degree. Two days later I get a phone call. Renovations are happening in the old section of a modern theatre and the building needs photo documentation for insurance.

'I'd been looking for a photographer and then your email miraculously appeared,' says the manager.

It's good timing and I'm hired. When I arrive, the manager sets up a ghost light for me, illuminating the haunting space. He explains a ghost light is there to light a theatre space so it's not completely pitch black. I think of actors accidentally falling into the orchestra pit. This part of the old theatre is the behind-the-scenes area where backdrops are painted, and where old dressing rooms live. He asks me how much I will charge, and I make up my price – it's not very high. I don't want to charge an exorbitant price on my first photo gig, as I am worried he'll choose someone else. Besides, I want to get started straight away. The space reminds me of my adventures prowling the Old Museum Building back in Brisbane; filled with stories waiting to be unearthed. I pad along rickety floorboards, stepping between dried pigeon droppings and years of dust. A painters' table is splattered in dried paint from its past life in scenic backdrops. A wooden ladder casts oblique shadows all the way to the roof. I focus the camera on what I initially think is a pile of white chalk, but bird skeletons appear through the viewfinder. I reel back. The bones are bleached white, picked clean.

I document everything from the rusted coat hangers to the yellowed newspaper clippings from past performances. Old addresses and phone numbers are scribbled on walls, graffiti dating back to 1984. In another room, paint trickles down high walls. I set the camera on the tripod and shine the torch against the wall to capture it all. Dust collects along my arms as I lean against the floor. I photograph and explore over two days, and each afternoon I lose track of time until night falls. I find parts of the wall where three layers of paint are revealed, repainted over the decades in different colours. By now, I have completed the brief for the theatre. Soon I will go home to edit the photographs and compile them on a CD for the manager. But I can't bring myself to leave just yet. I can't resist taking a series of self-portraits in the space, over long exposures, just for myself.

With no one watching me, I feel free. I become an actor in parallel to the actors in the theatre elsewhere in the building. I move for the camera, again using the light from my own torch. Away from the ghost light, I position my camera up a flight of stairs, then run down to touch doorways as though opening them, while disappearing from the shutter's eye, ghostlike. Doing a photoshoot like this requires energy. I half-climb ladders, move rivers of blue tarpaulin with my arms to form a sea, bury myself in piles of shattered stage lights while being careful not to cut myself on broken glass shards. I press myself against walls, trying not to twist my ankle through the holes in the floor. I peer through the gaps and pulleys to levels far below. I dance, and move, and twirl. When I get home I ache, but it's a good feeling, like I've been working my creativity as well as the muscles in my body. I call the series of self-portraits 'When the Ghost Light Sings'.

Before \ Night stitching / 2011

By now a month has passed and it is May. When I am not dreaming of being a theatre photographer, I dream about being a film stills photographer. I complete another online search and discover an opportunity to volunteer on a set of student films. The crewing information night is happening in two days' time. At the crewing night, everyone looks creative – an abundance of curly hair, coloured knitted jumpers, scarves, and berets. I soak up the energy. The students who pitch their films promise accommodation on the Great Ocean Road; regional Victoria in the snow and amazing locations and effects. There are many films to choose from, each with their own allure. They all promise food: for the Chinese film, all the Chinese food you can eat; for the Iranian film they offer a banquet; the Italian film student offers up her mother's cooking.

At the end of the night, I head straight to Chinatown and find my favourite dumpling restaurant. It's open until 10pm. For $6.80, I order a bowl of vegetarian dumplings with mushroom, tofu, greens, and noodles in soup. The bowl is bigger than my head. Tonight, I finish it all, while circling what films I want to work on. I feel inspired and imagine seeing the Great Ocean Road for the first time. I head for the train, the list of films clutched in my hand.

On the train ride home, one man picks up another man and slams him into the train window. I move into the next carriage and press the emergency button, skin on fire and alert, ready for battle. There's no security guard in sight. I see a punch thrown and more people cram into my carriage, away from the men. I decide to get off at an earlier stop. I glimpse a man's face with spots of blood, flashes of yellow from a Hawks scarf.

I wait for the next train to take me home, feeling unsafe. I remember an emailed invite to a party at a nightclub for young Jewish people. Because I'd hopped off at the earlier stop, it's nearby. I decide to get my mojo back. I've never set foot in a nightclub but surely it must be safer than the streets. Inside, the floor sticks to my shoes and it's muggy.

'Take off your jacket! Are you religious or something?' a guy on the dance floor yells at me.

I take a deep breath and scurry to the bathroom; sit on the couch just inside. A girl comes out of a toilet cubicle and washes her hands at the sink. I try to remain inconspicuous, but the girl picks up on my mood.

'Nice dress – you okay?'

'Yeah, but I'm thinking of going home now,' I say, deciding that I've had enough excitement for one night.

'Stay for a bit longer, you only just got here,' the girl says, dragging me out to the bar.

'I picked her up in the bathroom!' I hear the girl say to the barman over the roaring music.

'Water?'

Another guy says something to me – I don't catch what he says, and he makes a face. The music is so loud it thuds through the floorboards and into my feet as though the stickiness of dried booze is the conductor allowing the current to flow. A cool glass of water finds its way into my hands, and I have the thought: my water is spiked. I put it back on the counter even though I am dying to take a sip, and make my way out of the nightclub, down the narrow staircase. I look at my map in the dark; consider walking home through several suburbs. There's a line of taxis and an even longer queue of people. It was a mistake coming to the nightclub. I don't fit in. The guy who made a face at me earlier follows behind.

'How long did you spend in there? Half an hour? Come by yourself?'

'Yeah.'

'Are you religious? You don't order kosher meat, do you?' he asks.

The house where I am renting a room belongs to a Jewish woman and has two separate sinks, one for washing up meat dishes and one for milk-based dishes. She has a strict kosher meat rule, which means I am only allowed to cook chicken that has been killed without pain and blessed by a rabbi. Kashrut. Technically I just buy the chicken in the kosher section at Coles and don't need to specially order it. But this seems like a long and complicated answer, so I just say, 'I don't eat ham or shellfish. But I like lasagne.'

'Ooh mixing milk and meat – naughty.'

He offers me a lift home. My hands feel like ice. I am exhausted and need the lift, figuring it is safer than catching the train where more punch-ups could happen, so I get into the boy's car. He tells me about his Jewish ancestry – his family is

Sephardi. He has dark hair and eyes, matching his leather jacket. I tell him my family escaped from Poland. When he stops outside my place, he asks for my number. I knew accepting the lift would have consequences. But I give him my number, say, 'Thanks, bye', and am out the door before he can try a move.

The next day I get a text from him. He says I seem cool, and would I like to catch up for a coffee? A coffee is not a possibility. There is no way I can meet with this boy. I panic about sending back a text. I try to think about my reasoning but simply know I feel too anxious to start a relationship with anyone. Besides, I hadn't felt any attraction to the boy and don't want the pressure of dating to get to know him better. I call Mum.

'Did you like him?' she asks.

'I just needed a lift home. I've made a terrible mistake. I don't know if I like him. Not particularly, I suppose.'

'You don't have to go out with someone if you don't want to, Anna.'

I craft my message to the boy, replying I've got too much volunteer work on. Send. Another text from him pops up. He wants me to let him know if I change my mind. It's the coldest day in May in Melbourne in more than a decade. I warm my hands with my hair dryer.

The text I sent about the volunteer work taking up my time was a lousy excuse but true. I have been accepted to volunteer at a Jewish Radio Station. When I called and explained to the radio station that I was a photographer, they'd said they needed some images for their website. The next morning, the air is crisp and leaves crunch under my feet. I am half an hour early, so I sit at a café and order a cheese puff Danish sprinkled with icing sugar. I drink two cups of green tea. The door opens; a woman comes in and orders a cheesecake for ten people. I finish my tea as another woman with a baby comes in – she orders rugelach, an almond puff, a poppy seed puff, a cherry puff and five falafels. I set out again. I ring the doorbell to the radio station. The man talks to his assistants in Hebrew before greeting me and introducing me to the others in English.

We walk past the radio studios. There are two rooms with a glass partition in between. We sit down and he shows me how to cut audio together. I get out my camera.

'The desk is the most important part of the station,' he says.

He points to a brick of dials, controls, and the compressor.

There are signs up around the room: 'Be careful what you say into the mike! Broadcasting Do Not Enter!' A segment begins and I photograph in between the recordings so as not to disturb them with the shutter noise. The timer counts backwards, and the Station ID fades in before and after each item.

'Now I'm going to normalise and hard limit the audio. Do you want to record a show as well as photograph?'

To record a radio show is secretly a dream come true. I had recorded pretend radio shows with Alan over Mum's old classical cassette tapes when I was ten, complete with ad breaks, musical interludes, news updates, weather reports, and sound effect segments using playbacks from a Yak Bak – my favourite '90s electronic recording toy – that could warp our voices. The Yak Bak and rectangular blue and white cassette player had been a portal of joy for many hours of 'The Anna and Alan Show'.

'Okay,' I say, and he whisks me into the other studio where two girls are chatting in Hebrew.

He shows me how to navigate the settings as we go along and then leaves me to record the rest of their pilot. I put the headphones on and try to remember what he has shown me. I turn the microphones up, read the levels and adjust the slides to make sure they're in the right range when they speak. I then turn the speakers down, insert the audio, fade in and out the Station IDs and layer the tracks so they flow seamlessly. The timer reads fifty-seven minutes and I've recorded a real radio show.

I tell him the show is now recorded, and he smiles and says: 'Tomorrow is a surprise for another of our presenters. Come early and bring your camera. It will be great.'

The next day I wake up and it's freezing – ten degrees. I warm my hands with my hair dryer again before sprinting the twenty minutes up the hill to the radio station, my camera bag hitting my leg with each step. I head up the fire escape to meet the first presenter. He carries a big cup of coffee in his hand and says he didn't get to sleep until two in the morning. His eyes are red, and he looks in no mood for a surprise. All he knows is that there's a guest speaker. We cram ourselves into the studio. He gives a professional good morning wrap, cuts to a song, and then turns off the microphones and talks to the other presenter.

'He should be here by now. We need a producer.'

'He'll be here, look, that's him.'

'Hi, I'm Ziek.'

Ziek's left hand supports a large yellow tub. The presenter flicks some switches back on.

'And we're live.'

'Now I see you've brought a yellow container with you. I didn't know this was show and tell. What's in the box?'

'Well, it contains a six-metre python and several other reptiles.'

'What? You mean there is a snake in that box in the studio?'

Ziek is a reptile expert.

'I'm not impressed; you know I have a fear of snakes,' the

presenter says as the snake uncoils across the desk. I focus the camera and snap away.

'And we have a live snake in the studio. How's that for a surprise on Erev Shavuot? Don't forget to eat your cheesecake tonight everyone!'

The festival of Shavuot marks the first Jewish anniversary, the Yahrzeit, of Nana's passing. That afternoon I sit in the garden before going to synagogue as doubt, anxiety, and depression wash over me. The weather propels me onwards; pushes as though agitated I might miss the old synagogue. Rich red carpet leads to a small area out the back. A table is laden with blintzes and thimbles of vodka. The rabbi sings a few prayers, and a gathering grows in the room beyond. I do not usually drink, except for a mouthful of kosher wine on religious festivals or Shabbat. On this night I take a sip of vodka, feeling its warmth in my chest. More blessings are said over the food, and I try to sing along to the Hebrew as I pile cream cheese blintzes filled with sultanas onto my plate. The talk is cheerful, and I think of my family, who would be attending my synagogue in Brisbane. I'd moved to Melbourne to experience more of my Jewish culture – but I miss my family and start to wonder what I am doing in this city, so far away.

I am feeling exhausted and can't make my way up the hill the following day. I decide to take the tram one stop but realise too late that the Metcard I got from one of the ticket officers at the train station has expired. I haven't used the machine on the tram before. I'm in the middle of the carriage trying to work it out as I'm jostled in everyone's way, and as it's only one stop there, I decide to sit down. As if on cue, ticket inspectors stop the tram and swoop in from outside. They corner me and I say this is my stop. They follow me off the tram and I sit on a bench overshadowed by a woman with a gold badge and hard blue eyes. A man in uniform stands behind her. Good cop bad cop.

'You'll have to show us something to verify your address,' she says to me.

'I don't have anything yet. I'm from Brisbane.'

'You need to verify your address, or the police will be involved.'

The guy is holding something – maybe a voice recorder.

'You have the right to remain silent.'

I give Dad's number and she talks to him. Then she gives me the phone and I hear his familiar voice.

'What's going on? Who was that woman?'

'I didn't know how to work the tram ticket machine in time. She's really rude.'

'Don't let it upset your day,' he says and hangs up.

I pass the woman's phone back.

'I wasn't being rude,' she says, her composure gone, voice angry.

'That was a personal call,' I say, which makes her face flash red, and I rally back with the violent train experience from the other week – how I'd pressed the emergency button and no security had appeared.

'That's not my area. I'm only in charge of this day. Expect a fine in the mail.'

The man gives me an apologetic look and they leave. I wait for my legs to regain their strength.

Because of this debacle I'm late to my volunteering at the radio station. Someone else is recording a show in my usual spot so I use the other studio. Time is running away, and the two women are waiting. One of them says she must leave for an interview at 11am. After I click the settings, which seem unfamiliar in this studio, I record them talking for twenty minutes. But when I recheck the soundtrack, to my dismay, I realise the recording hasn't worked. I tell them that we'll have to do it again next time. The girls are kind, saying it's not my fault. At home I dissolve in tears. To make myself feel better I head out to take some photographs of the ruins at the museum. It has rained the night before and dirty water floats in the cracks and crevices of the old sculptures. What was once an adventure in Melbourne starts to unwind and unravel, like a pulled thread, catching on small events.

There's an exhibition I want to see at a gallery, and I embark on a journey to find it. I become lost and spend three hours trying to find the show on foot. When I finally arrive at the gallery, I am unable to keep still or concentrate, and barely look at the artworks. That afternoon I arrive home to find my tram fine in the mail, which is in the vicinity of $300. I don't want any trouble so I pay, even though Dad has said he could help me write a letter to contest it. I throw myself into the weather, walk down dark rainy streets, grateful for my gumboots as icy rain lashes. Another theatre has written back to me, saying that while they can't offer me paid work, I can volunteer. So tonight, I am volunteering to photograph a dress rehearsal, shadowing their main photographer. I am early and sit on the stairs leading up to the theatre, waiting for the doors to open as rain slants diagonally. A woman walks past and says I can shelter and read in her artist library next door. She seems concerned for me, or suspicious. I can't tell which.

When the woman turns on the heaters, I realise I have landed myself in the middle of a nude drawing class. I focus on the books of watercolours. When it's time for the theatre to open I slip away from the artist's library and head to the theatre stalls. My reflexes are quick as I capture the actors' expressions. I keep out of the main photographer's way – he takes the left side of the theatre and I focus on the right. I seem to sense where each expression will land as I take the shot. The wind howls when I return home. I lose my keys – then find them under the tripod.

The next day, I sit in a café to warm myself up and order an apricot custard Danish, a twisted pastry, and one jam doughnut. Despite all the food, my watch is feeling looser. There is so much challah everywhere. There's pain under my arm, and my feet feel sprained from walking in gumboots. I don't know whether I'm having a nervous breakdown or a panic attack. I can sense something bad is coming – something not quite right. The feeling roils towards me, a premonition. The memories become harder to remember. A man hands me a stack of books after a writing workshop I have participated in. He seems concerned for me – keeps giving me writing anthologies, piling them in my arms as though wanting to make me feel better, until I have to say I can't carry them all back with me. I walk home and as I sit huddled on the floor, I can almost see something flickering on the horizon outside my window – perhaps the Grim from *Harry Potter*, a large black dog – the omen of death. Something is coming for me, and I don't know what.

I look up flights and start to pack. There's one cheaper flight out of all the expensive ones and it seems to be a sign. I book my flight home. The opportunity to volunteer as a film stills photographer along the Great Ocean Road slips away. I can't work out what is happening to me, when things seemed to go so well with documenting the old theatre. I had been planning to at least stay until the exhibition of three of my photographs in a local gallery, that was scheduled for the end of the week. The tram fine upset me more than it should have. No, there is something Other at play now. Something is happening that I cannot control, and I don't know what it is.

The cat belonging to the house where I am renting a room has glared at me for my entire seven-week-stay. The cat now comes and sits on my chest as I lie on the floor. It too senses something is wrong. Arrives to my aid too late. My memories falter. *The howling wind*, I write in a notebook, *I cannot sleep with the wind*. I manage to catch the flight home to Brisbane. I have bags upon bags with me. I wear my sunglasses even though it is night. I have layered most of my clothes over me to save on packing space. I am wearing at least three heavily padded jumpers and look like a matzah ball dumpling. These memories of my arrival appear from a distance, as though I'm looking down the wrong end of a telescope, taking me further away from myself.

I do not remember my week in Brisbane before the madness consumes me. The only evidence of my existence is on my hard drive, in the photographs and videos I took during the seven days. There are clues as to my leaving this self, the transition to my splitting. On returning home to Brisbane, I become fixated with documenting the rooms in my family home as though I have never seen them before: the lounge room, the kitchen. I take many photographs of a blue papier mâché mask I'd once made in art class as a teenager. I recall the mask had taken me time to make; I'd spent the three-hour class finessing it, edging the cut-out eyes with golden dust, swirling the glue so the glitter would stick to the blue feathers at the crown. A pale blue wishing stone obscured the place where a third eye might open. Could the mask's third eye see something I could not?

I know I visit a café with Grandad the next day, because I take many portraits of him and his steak sandwich with chips, as though I am trying to fix his memory in place with each photo. He has always loved steak sandwiches – this is family legend. He loves them even more in later years as a reprieve from the soft nursing home food. I feel the need to capture Grandad and his sandwich in as many frames as possible. I zoom in on his grinning face by moving my camera, until his eyes become alarmed at the closeness of the shutter. The following day I am at the art gallery café with Mum and my chai latte. Though smiling, Mum too has a concerned look in her eyes, trying to work out what is wrong by peering through the lens at me. Every time I revisit a photograph of Mum from during this week, she has this look. It's as though she can sense something is amiss but does not know exactly what.

I must have developed my film from Melbourne the minute I returned to Brisbane, because the rolls are scanned and date-stamped on my computer, again linked to that week. I have scanned the film carefully in the film holders at a high resolution. In roll one, Melbourne and its autumn leaves swirl across the square medium format film, containing the odd light that glows before a storm, and the ruins by the museum. Roll two contains wrought iron on buildings so fine it looks like lattice, and a lake I now have no memory of visiting. Roll three is a series of poisonous red mushrooms with white spots, growing next to a suspended lamp as though transported from a European fairy tale.

I do not remember catching up with my friends Anne and Charlotte that week, but there is footage of us together in front of an ice-skating rink set up inexplicably in King George Square. I am fascinated by the professional ice-skating show – the videos I take span minutes. I try to catch every jump and twirl of the skaters, as though I am the official sports photographer. I can sense my friends watching and wondering when we can move on to the shops. We go to a movie together later that night – *Jane Eyre*. I come away from it feeling overwhelmed and depressed in mood. My reaction is too intense, and I know I have become too invested in the film and cannot separate myself from the main character. To this day, I cannot comfortably watch movies or television programs with others, tendrils from this week still appearing in my life.

During that week, I'd also taken self-portraits in the Photo Booth app on my computer. These images reveal themselves like a mood journal. In my self-portraits the darkness under my eyes extends to my cheekbones. My face looks so tired it appears bruised. In one series I wear a purple beret I brought back from Melbourne and pose, pursing my lips. In the next day's self-portraits, I let the sun stream through the window and wash out my face so all that's left is an oval of white, no markings of self, only my long, curly brown hair on either side of nothingness. The computer's inbuilt camera cannot register my features with all the light. This series of images leads into the night of my madness. I do remember sitting in front of the computer and creating these portraits, but don't recognise that I'd tipped into madness by this point. I'd used the temperature filter – red pounds across the screen the closer I move my body to the camera. My fingers contort like a magician. My expression is blank in these images, my face blue and green and distanced from the red of my hands. In the next series I hold my djembe drum. There is a video sequence of me playing the drum. My expression is animated but exaggerated, as though I'm running a demonstration for *Play School*.

Alan can tell something is wrong instantly when he sees me in the study. I do not have any memories of these sequences of events but he will later tell me the following: I am bizarrely dressed and my bag is packed. I say I will save the family by going into the forest. I am ready to go and he asks me to wait, just to stop me from leaving the house. He finds Mum and Dad, who are watching TV, and says 'something is wrong with Anna'.

Mum and Alan take it in turns to watch me, and talk with me. Alan shows me some comedy on television. I cannot understand why everyone is laughing onscreen, but I am distracted from my quest – my brother has saved my life.

As soon as the GP's practice opens early the next morning, Dad drives me there with Mum and Alan for assistance. Later, my GP will tell me how I'd made a call to her the night I went mad. She will tell me that my message was garbled and filled with static but full of need. She says I was trying to tell her what was wrong but couldn't get the words out. She hadn't been able to call me back because I'd rung from the private home phone and not my mobile and she didn't have access to my number. When our car pulls up to the car park, my GP rushes out from seeing her list of patients for the day. She climbs into the backseat of the car to sit with me, tablet in hand. But I ignore the tablet and start stroking her long hair. A queue of patients is waiting to see her. She wants me to take the tablet, but I am still stroking her hair. When she realises that nothing more can be done, my family then drives me to the hospital on her instructions. My parents coax me into a wheelchair at the hospital because I refuse to walk. I will later be transferred from this hospital to another hospital. These are the snippets that have been told to me by others.

Years later Alan will tell me about another missing piece in my memory. How I hadn't wanted to let go of his jumper when he'd wheeled me into the hospital, and he'd had to remove the jumper to get free from my strong grip. Mum, Dad, and Alan had walked into a busy hospital emergency room. The man on the desk was overwhelmed and had not wanted to let me in – he didn't realise how unwell I was. Mum gave the man her phone with my GP on the end of the line – soon after, his expression changed, and we were in a room with a doctor. The doctor told my family to go. Alan had walked out last, and the door was shut. Alan tells me I had then pressed my face and hands in the small glass window of the door, looking at him with big eyes, saying, 'Help, Alan, help.'

'Go!' the doctor had yelled to Alan.

I had no idea until Alan tells me these details about how painful it must have been for him.

Soon after, my family saw two big guards running through the hospital.

'That's for Anna,' my brother had said.

Perhaps those had been the very two guards who had stopped me from escaping the ward, when the door had slammed on my finger, giving me my scar. Mum will later tell me I booked twenty psychology appointments during the week in the lead-up to my madness that she'd had to cancel, and that I was crying the night I went mad. I knew I was desperate for help, that something was very wrong. I was distressed because I couldn't see Mum's arms and hands. It was as if her hands vanished when I looked at her – she kept showing me that her hands were there, but I couldn't see them. Alan stayed up with me for the rest of the night because I could see him whole.

What does it mean to not remember that week myself before my madness hit? It means a gap, a black hole, a split in self. There is nothing I can do about it. No prompting can bring it back. It is gone. I had no say. I know I should be grateful for the abyss that obliterated memories of deep trauma. But where did that trauma go? A girl still experienced it. She just doesn't remember. I have lost part of my life's knowledge. While I understand that memory loss is its own lived experience, I want to know what it was like to have crossed into the realm of madness. After all, I did it. I went mad. Why can't I have the secret knowledge that comes with it? All I have are its rough edges. I have always wondered what I would have done had I propelled myself into the Mount Coot-tha Forest. There were no scattered notes left for me to work out what path I would have taken, whether it be the Honey Eater track to the Lookout, or even all the way to JC Slaughter Falls, the most haunted track of Mount Coot-tha. Perhaps there would have been more ghosts by the end of my journey had no one found me in time.

I took over seven thousand photographs in 2011 and felt like I documented each moment. It's as though I knew I would need to capture as much as possible so I could piece myself back together again. What was once passion tipped into obsession. I have never taken that many photographs in a single year since. Who was this girl who had a camera attached to her hand in the street? This girl who needed to document each sign and interaction, taking photo after photo without pause. I can see her as if from a distance, from the other side of the split. In my photographs I can almost see my self leaving her as she becomes her own character, a doubling of selves. There's something about the intensity of her eyes and the darkness under them. She's someone I don't recognise. Someone lost. Someone Other. But she's also someone I will cross paths with when I feel myself ease back into consciousness. As I return to my body over the year after my madness, I now realise Cardea was still there too. I will not feel like I'm in my own body again for a long time. I am co-existing with her: Cardea, the hinge between my past and present selves.

Cardea \ Glow-in-the-dark knitting needles / 2011–2012

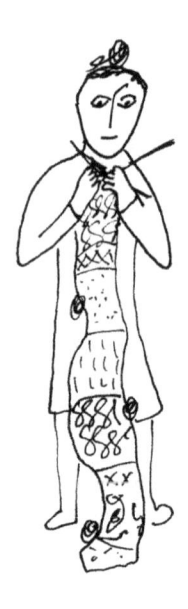

During the year after she is released from hospital, remnants from her madness continue to surprise her. When she wakes one morning and opens her eyes, a whale she has dreamt of continues to swim across her wall in halo-yellow, then fades with a wave of its tail into the distance and is gone. It's as though she has glimpsed her dream's aura floating through the waking world. One afternoon, when she looks out the bus window as it comes to a stop at traffic lights, the road moves like a river of tar. She watches as the tar glides into the distance like a perspective shift gone wrong. The longer the bus sits at the lights, the road's shifting begins to settle like a droplet of water coming to rest, until it is still. She tells all this to her psychiatrist, James, who notes it down and says not to worry; she has insight, and the visions will go with time.

Driving is difficult for her since the memory loss. She needs to renavigate the once-familiar streets and rebuild the maps she had known without looking. She is uncertain walking around the block. On one such walk she and Alan had discovered the communal mulberry tree near their home. They'd savoured two ripe berries picked high up in the branches, washed clean with a little water from their drink bottles. But without Alan beside her, she doubts she'd find her way home again. She feels lost at sea, barely two streets from her home. She used to be able to drive to all her friends' houses and now the anxiety at the thought of driving wraps itself around the visit. When her friend Nadia invites her to a crafternoon, where she will meet up with all her old friends as a group since her hospitalisation for the first time, the very real problem she foresees is how to get there. She feels that if she can't make this trip by herself, and relies on others to ferry her about, she will lose her independence.

She has retained a sense of the way to Nadia's house in her head; it's a fifteen-minute drive but she'd have to travel along the Western Freeway and go through a roundabout. James has warned her that if she doesn't get back into driving, the circle of places she can drive to will get smaller and smaller. Her case manager, Stephanie, refused to understand why she'd lost confidence in driving since the psychosis, and she hopes James will not be the same. When she explains more of her predicament to James, he tells her a story. How one time, he avoided going through tunnels because he'd gotten stuck there the previous day due to a traffic incident. But then he realised that if it was tunnels, what would it be next? He decided to go through at least one tunnel every day and expose himself to the fear. He says at first it felt like torture, but by the end he was able to drive through tunnels.

The next day, she gets in the family car and drives to Indooroopilly Shopping Centre. James has said it would be best for her to start off with driving short distances to places she knows and then broaden where she can go. She concentrates on relaxing her shoulders and her grip on the steering wheel. She does a loop of the car park, returns a library book, then comes home again in one piece. The tension has bunched up in her muscles and she is as stiff and sore as when she first had driving lessons as a teenager.

The day of the crafternoon arrives. She knows she is a careful driver, and this helps steady her nerves and give her confidence. The ride goes smoothly until her anxiety hits on the freeway, and she feels like she's going to faint. She takes deep breaths and switches on the radio to drown out her thoughts. The music helps, and when she parks outside Nadia's house, she feels a huge sense of achievement.

'Anna, it's so great to see you.'

'You too.'

She's never been to a crafternoon before, and Nadia teaches her how to knit. The first two rows take all her concentration, and she drops a few stitches. Once she settles into a rhythm, she falls into a meditative state, watching her hands knit as if from a distance. Her knitting looks like a ragged boot, instead of a scarf, but she's getting the hang of the basic knitting stitch. The conversation washes over her until Nadia says, 'I think it's time for cake. Who wants tea?'

The sponge cake is filled with apple and apricots, dusted with icing sugar. She eats one piece, which disappears so quickly she decides to have another one to make up for it. She stops herself from devouring the whole cake by focusing on the knitting. Her medication makes her crave sweet carbohydrates and she's put on fifteen kilograms since her time in hospital.

'So how was Melbourne?' asks Nadia.

She pauses in her knitting. She still can't remember any details from her Melbourne trip.

'You were brave going in winter,' Nadia says.

'Yeah.'

She lets the subject drop like a stitch, and they move on to another thread. Her friends don't push her, they accept her quirks. Just by spending time with them again, she feels she is knitting herself back into her friendship group; the gap left by her absence nearly forgotten.

The crafternoons continue with her friends over the following months. Nadia has progressed to crochet, granny-square blankets, and cushion covers, while she's still knitting the same scarf with the spare coloured yarns her friends have gifted her. But she doesn't mind – having grasped the basic stitch is enough for her. Her friends say her scarf is 'eclectic' and 'wonderfully unusual' as encouragement. When she feels like adding more to her handiwork, she continues her knitting at home, working out ways to fill the misshapen holes by making bright pompoms. The process of creating through knitting gives her inspiration to write new stories, and they align more closely to her frame of mind than she realises. In her stories, scarves grow from one-and-a-half metres to twenty. Yarn fills the rooms in houses. Thoughts wind themselves into her stitches. She teaches creatures to knit their memories. Memories spool onto needles and into thread, becoming cloaks and gloves.

She is tying on a luminous green pompom to hide a large hole in her scarf when she receives a call that a space has opened at Mind Gym – the program James first recommended to help with her memory.

She makes her way to Fortitude Valley by train and waits for her fellow participants. Inside the clinic, a homeless-looking man watches the television screen bolted into the ceiling: *Days of Our Lives*.

'Comes in at this time every day for that show,' she hears one receptionist tell the other from behind the glass. She's been told that Mind Gym participants have all experienced some form of psychosis and she is nervous. She does a lap of the chairs, pacing.

'Glad I'm not the only fruitcake on the planet,' a man says to her on his way to reception, his appointment over. By being here, she is lumped in like dried fruit – sultanas, orange rind, and glacé cherries – into the realm of those who've tasted madness. Finally, another man with wiry glasses and a swinging lanyard unlocks the door to the Mind Gym room with a bunch of keys. Inside, the half-dozen ancient machines remind her of her family's first computer from 1996, even though it's now 2012.

'These have been donated due to funding issues, but still work well,' says the facilitator, patting one of the computers. She sits at a boxy computer and is surprised it turns on when she presses the button. There is no one else her age in the group here, which makes her feel like an anomaly. The woman sitting to her left is missing teeth. The man to her right wears an eyepatch. They are both getting through the games faster than she is. Seeing no other representation for people who have had psychosis, she worries she too will inevitably lose teeth, become homeless, and gain an eye patch if she has episode after episode. At the end of the hour-long session, they gather around a table and the facilitator clears his throat.

'Now, we're going to talk about memory. Does anyone know what tools they might use to help with remembering things?'

'I try not to remember. I use cannabis,' says the woman with missing teeth.

'Okay, well yes, you can discuss that in your other group. Anyone else?'

The facilitator looks at her. She doesn't want to speak, but there is one thing which has helped her over the past year. She says she uses a diary, and he exclaims in recognition and writes the word 'diary' on the whiteboard. He gives a talk about the importance of a diary for memory, and then gets down to the business of shuffling a pack of Uno cards. She loses every round.

Once or twice, she thinks she sees Katie from her old hospital ward walking through the city but cannot be sure. In hospital she had thought Katie was ten but was later told she was sixteen. Katie is tiny, made up of fragments of energy, fragments of fragments. One day, at the King George bus stop, Katie smiles at her in recognition, even though she cannot be sure it is really her. She smiles back. The bus pulls up. Katie does not say anything and neither does she. She gets on the bus.

The side effects from the medications won't go away: tremors still shake her hands when she uses a fork to eat, her exhaustion contrasts with a restlessness that makes it unbearable to sit still. She feels let down by her body, her brain. Her doctor has told her things to look out for in case of another episode: paranoia, not sleeping, hearing voices. She wonders whether she will be able to recognise the signs and be aware next time. It seems outside of her control. Her memories stop where the madness began – as if there had been no warning.

Usually after an episode of psychosis people become depressed. James's words float back to her. If anything is making her depressed, it's her case manager and all the hospital visits for her appointments each week. Although James is a wonderful doctor, setting foot in the hospital waiting room again is enough to bring her down. She stays in bed for hours at a time, unable to summon the energy to get herself going. When she walks to the café with Mum, she finds herself staring into the distance and the conversation is one-sided. She tries to meet Mum's eyes but can't seem to lift her vision above the table. She tells Mum she feels like crap. That it's appointment after appointment. It's like she's sliding sideways on the better scale. Not heading up or down. She doesn't want to start on an antidepressant or be on medication and seeing psychiatrists and case managers every week and realises she'll always be looking over her shoulder for the psychosis beast because of what inevitably follows – a hospitalisation within a mental health care system that takes away her rights. She wipes away angry tears as Mum holds her hand.

'It's just hit you what's happened, hasn't it?'

'Yeah.'

Band rehearsals are not going well. The side effects from her antipsychotic leave her with a lip tremor when playing the French horn. This makes the notes sound wobbly with a constant vibrato. It's a weird sensation – like the hand tremor that she's now used to, but across her lips. She swaps her fourth part for the higher second part with one of the other horns, as the lower notes seem to make the tremor worse. Usually playing her

French horn makes her feel better but now she is so down she can barely raise the instrument when she practises at home, let alone gather the air to play a note. The only thing that makes rehearsals worthwhile is the Old Museum Building that still stands like a castle along Gregory Terrace.

Tonight, at band rehearsal, it's so hot the side doors are pushed wide open and the screech of bats creates a cacophony. Beyond the conductor rise giant Narnian cupboards and timber cabinets from the building's past life as the museum. Stained glass ripples like an oil slick against the night and if she cranes her neck back, she can see the ceiling rise into a peak, high above. Rehearsals at the Old Museum Building are filled with the possibilities of a discovery. In the backstage corridors, empty double bass cases string along the walls like black coffins and she hears the melodies of another orchestra rehearsing in the Concert Hall. The walls pinch the sounds and tuck them into the bricks, choosing musical phrases at will.

But this year, lasting through a whole rehearsal has become difficult. She no longer has the stamina she'd built up after fifteen years of playing, and concert nights have felt different for her. It's not just performance anxiety that she feels – something else is stirring. She walks onto the stage with the other horns, not looking at the audience but hearing them rustle and clap and murmur. Her face heats up under the watch of so many eyes, even though she cannot see them in the darkness that falls beyond the stage. She tries to concentrate on the music, on following the repeats and using dynamics but she keeps running out of air for the crescendos. Usually, her fingers just fly by themselves but now they are clumsy and slow. Even though she is in a band of forty musicians, with three other powerful horn players, she senses the audience hone in on her sound. She feels like a fraud. She used to see the horn as an extension of herself: a proper mouthpiece. Its call was clear and carried across the room. The instrument had represented dedication to her practice, her musicality and creativity: she had even won the National Open French Horn championship just four years ago. But something has shifted.

These past months she has not practised the pieces during the week between rehearsals, not liking the feeling of the lip tremor and unintended vibrato. Even when she's tried to lift the horn from its velvet-lined case, it has seemed too heavy. After the last concert for the year, she leaves the band. She keeps her French horn in its case, wedged into the bottom of the cupboard. After not being able to lift the French horn because of the weight of her mood, she knows that something must change. She tells James that she'll try the antidepressant, feeling like she is surrendering her life. She can only focus on his neat black shoe as he writes out a script. She follows the instructions and swallows the meds at night. She waits for the common side effects the pamphlet lists – headache, nausea, stomach problems. But other side effects strike in unexpected ways. After a visit to Indooroopilly Shopping Centre, she is crossing the road as usual to get to the other side. As she reaches the middle of the road, she cannot force her legs to move. It's as though the message to walk from her brain to her legs has scrambled. The lights change as she tries to propel herself, in jerky movements, to the other side of the road, watching as though from above. She feels the metal breath of cars zoom past, almost touching her.

When she tells James, he says to discontinue the antidepressant by decreasing it slowly and starting gradually with another. The next medication makes the world look like it's an underwater blur, even with her glasses on. Her hands shake so hard she can barely write her own name or use a spoon. When she is given another to try, she feels like a science experiment and not in control of her life. She is severely fatigued on the third antidepressant and now has limited energy, but the threads start weaving her bones back into her skin. James ups the dosage. The threads weave faster.

Cardea \ A stitch in time saves nine / 2012–2013

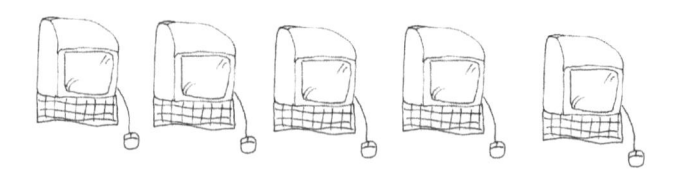

Each week she progresses to higher levels of the Mind Gym memory games. In one game, squares of colours appear on screen, and she remembers the sequence and repeats them. They flash rapidly – the longer the sequence, the harder it becomes, until she can repeat up to ten different colours.

Magenta
Click
Magenta Orange
Click Click
Magenta Orange Aqua
Click Click Click
Magenta Orange Aqua Red
Click Click Click Click
Magenta Orange Aqua Red Purple
Click Click Click Click Click
Magenta Orange Aqua Red Purple Orange
Click Click Click Click Click Click
Magenta Orange Aqua Red Purple Orange Indigo
Click Click Click Click Click Click Click
Magenta Orange Aqua Red Purple Orange Indigo Yellow
Click Click Click Click Click Click Click Click
Magenta Orange Aqua Red Purple Orange Indigo Yellow Magenta
Click Click Click Click Click Click Click Click Click
Magenta Orange Aqua Red Purple Orange Indigo Yellow Magenta Brown
Click Click Click Click Click Click Click Click Click Click

'What level are you up to?' asks the facilitator.

She tells him she's reached level ten, and he looks surprised.

'I couldn't get past level seven – that's amazing.'

She is sure this isn't true and that he is just trying to make her feel better. Besides, the memory games are ones that children play. But slowly, she can feel her concentration begin to improve. She is even able to read again and finds all the literature she can, written by women who have experienced either psychosis or hospitalisations or both. With her renewed ability to concentrate once more, she reads *Flying with Paper Wings* by Sandy Jeffs, *An Unquiet Mind* by Kay Redfield Jamison, *Madness: A Memoir* by Kate Richards, and *An Angel At My Table* by Janet Frame. She also discovers Elmo Keep's *Meanjin* piece 'Summer and Antipsychotics in the City'. These resilient women remember most of their experiences and write with clarity. But because she can't remember her madness, she feels cheated out of her own experience.

She has managed to attend every single session over the twenty weeks of Mind Gym. During the last session, Sam ruffles his hands through the test papers.

'We're going to see how much you've improved from the beginning of the course. You may not remember this test as we did it soon after you got out of hospital.'

The facilitator must be mistaken – she was never given such a test. Though she knows she has probably forgotten it.

'I need you to name as many things as you can starting with the letter "S". This will test your long-term memory.'

She tries to focus.

'Your time starts – now.'

'Snarl, secret, serpent, sin.'

She feels ridiculous; she wants to do well.

'Sun, summer, sultana, sultry, sunburn, salt, savoury, salvage, sizzle.'

She stumbles over words.

'Space, snake, saucer, scare.'

She is careful not to say the word 'sex'. She doesn't want Sam to think she's got sex on the brain. She doesn't want to see the 'gotcha' expression on his face. She realises she's being irrational. She realises she's stopped speaking. She thinks: shit.

'Sick, six, sabotage, septicemia.'

Sam frowns at 'septicemia'. Definitely do not say 'sex' and 'shit'. Do not say—

'Time's up.'

One week passes before she gets the phone call to say her memory has improved in all the areas tested. She puts down the phone, relieved. Even without the call she knows she's getting better. Although her memory from her madness is a roll of film that refuses to develop, her hands are no longer pushing at brick as she tries to access her Melbourne memories from the past year. The barrier – woven strong with its own hair-reinforced concrete – is crumbling.

With the return of her Melbourne memories, poetry pours down her arms and into the keyboard. She catches the bus to the library and borrows books of poetry. She doesn't just want to try and read them; she wants to see what a book of poetry looks like, how it's ordered, the number of pages and how it's all put together. She wants to make a book of her own poetry and photographs. Sitting in her study, she is grateful for the room Mum set up for her. It used to contain a fort of things: bags of old clothes, cupboards that refused to close, an old bed. Now it contains a desk for her computer and several bookshelves filled with photo albums. The winter sun through the window warms her as she writes. She still can't draw like she used to, but poetry has become vital as her new form of expression. She gathers her poems together in one document and titles her booklet of poetry *The Last Postman*. In the title poem, one of the first poems she has written, the world is surreal and includes a girl whose self splits.

> The girl sitting opposite shuffles her feet
> and looks at the planets.
> 'I don't know how I got here,' she says.
> 'Easy, you're the last postman –
> it's your ticket here.' He hands her the bag
> filled with fifteen letters, disappears
> out the closing doors.
>
> She knows that this is what called her
> to the train tonight. So she splits
> herself in fifteen different ways, follows
> the letters' separate paths.

She heads to the print shop, but doesn't tell Mum, wanting to surprise her with her creation. They print it on the spot for her and when she opens the paper bag, there it is: a hard copy of her poetry booklet, thermal bound. When she gets home, she shows the booklet to Mum.

'When did you do this?' she says, astonished. 'It's brilliant – we have to organise a colour copy.'

She keeps her poetry booklet in her top drawer, to flick through when she feels down. One day she wants to publish her work.

Six months after her hospitalisation, James encourages her to return to work or study. Mum looks up a course and writes it on a sticky note for her to consider: *Creative and Professional Writing*. Mum tells her she has noticed she has been writing more lately and is impressed with her poetry booklet. She reads the course description and looks at some of the units: Poetry, Short Story, Novel and Memoir. This is what she wants to do. Just as she had been driven to study photography all those years ago, to open more of that world to her eye, now she wants to learn all she can about writing. In a flurry she fills out the forms as best she can and the next morning, she catches the bus with Mum into uni with her application in hand. She feels embarrassed that she needs her mum as her support today, seeing as she managed the first time around by herself. She wonders if anyone else takes their mum with them to university. But she has been robbed of her confidence. Together, they navigate the staircase to the student services block and pay the late fee – today is the very last day to apply.

Two and a half weeks later she opens her email.

'Dear Anna, I am pleased to advise that your application for admission has been successful.'

And so, still dealing with the anxiety and depression left over from the psychosis and hospitalisation, she turns up at her first lecture to start another degree, this time in creative writing. Just six months after her hospitalisation, she is back in a university. She uses the visual diaries she was given in hospital for her notes and makes sure to rip out her therapy drawings before she attends her first lecture. She sits next to a girl with purple hair.

In a lecture on the horror genre, the lecturer asks them what they most fear. A girl puts up her hand and says, 'psychosis'. She hasn't noticed the girl before – she's not in her tutorial. Later, in the push-shove to get home, the girl vanishes. Her answer is all she will remember from the fifty-minute lecture. At home, she keeps her digital files in meticulous order on her hard drive because she knows that if psychosis happens again, everything will have to be clearly labelled for her to find things. She does not take memory and sanity for granted. She does not take anything for granted.

Her life from the past year folds into itself like lumpy cake batter filled with air pockets; a floury mess of memory and thought. She tries to complete her tutorial readings but feels expelled from the feast. Tutorial questions in class braid themselves into fat loaves and she cannot follow the three plaits that form their complex pattern of question, answer, and discussion. She smiles at her classmates, doing her best to appear normal, as anxiety empties her mind.

One lecturer gives a talk on writing as therapy and discusses the link between creativity and mental illness. This time, she feels right at home. In her uni breaks, she catches the bus to the hospital for her psychiatric appointments with James, only a couple of stops away from the campus on the busway. She is unsure if she will be able to keep up with the workload even part-time and with no job. But she starts her assignments early and finishes them weeks before the due date, so she won't get too stressed or panicked. She writes three short stories to choose from when she just needs one.

The first time she hands in one of her assignments, she checks it's in the document wallet at least five times. She staples on the cover sheet that she's printed out weeks in advance. She wraps the whole thing in a plastic bag in case it rains, even though the sun is throwing out light by the handful. When she finally gets to uni, days before the deadline, she checks another three times that her assignment is safe inside its folder, worried the pages have fallen out. She carefully hands the folder to the girl at Assignment Minder as though it contains one of Nana's porcelain plates. Scowling, the girl snatches the folder from her hands, scans it and throws it on the pile of assignments waiting for sorting. She sits in the library and checks her email to make sure it's been scanned properly. Relief pours through her when she sees the Assignment Minder notification. She goes through this routine every time an assignment is due. It seems the hardest part for her is not the writing of the assignment but its physical handing-in.

Her case manager Stephanie quits, and she is given a new case manager who gives her a series of IQ tests. It feels strange to be doing IQ tests while trying to complete her creative writing course. The case manager doesn't go into detail about her results but says she has scored below average in most of the categories. The old-fashioned questions like 'what does it mean to put a cat among the pigeons?' and 'a stitch in time saves nine' hadn't seemed an accurate way to define her intelligence, so she isn't too worried. Besides, it's her university marks that matter most to her and the end of semester is approaching.

In her last lecture, the lecturer reads out Sylvia Plath's experience with ECT as an example of description in creative writing. She borrows her book *The Bell Jar* from the library and reads it cover to cover. She is glad that there is no crackling blue light or bones exploding with metaphorical tree sap in her own experience of ECT. She tries writing about her madness in third-person short stories she shows no one. The psychosis theme has many incarnations in her work, but she feels she can never get it quite right. When she logs on to check her grades, she sees that in her first year of study, she has achieved three high distinctions and a credit, and is awarded a place on the Dean's List for academic performance. She knows she shouldn't have to prove anything to herself, but she's profoundly relieved she can do this 'going back to uni' thing and do it well. The university asks if she'd like to be a note-taker for the Equity and Disability services. She says yes, pleased that she's now able to help others.

She had never signed up for help from the Equity and Disability services, even though she would have qualified. She wants to know she can do this on her own terms and if this means proving something to herself, then so be it. She does not want to need help; she wants to be the helper. Besides, she isn't yet ready to disclose to an organisation that she has a disability.

Her weight has increased dramatically from her medications to the extent that she decides to try an all-women's gym with Mum. Before she can set foot on the machines, she is interrogated.

'What exercise have you been doing?' asks the instructor.

'Some walking,' she says.

The instructor writes 'couch potato' with five exclamation marks on the form and gives her a challenging look.

'Right, now for your weight and measurements.'

She checks her blood pressure and weight, and measures her height. She feels the measuring tape circle around her waist, hips, arms, and legs. Finally, the onslaught stops.

'Okay, now let's get you onto the circuit and we'll show you how to use the machines.'

She shows her the equipment and it's a montage of pushing and pulling, getting on and off, keeping her elbows bent at shoulder height, and then straightened. By the end of the circuit her heart rate is up, exhaustion has hit, and the instructor tosses her a towel.

'Good, Anna. Now I want you to come back at least three times a week and you'll soon feel a difference.'

'Come over for a movie night,' says Anne.
'Would you like me to bring anything?'
'Ice cream, please!'
She stands in front of the freezer doors, deliberating on rum and raisin ice cream or chocolate chip. It seems an important decision, and she lets the cool air from the refrigerator shelves wrap around her for a few moments, as she compares price and flavour. Just as she's decided to go for the all-favourite chocolate chip and is reaching out a hand, she hears a voice say, 'Oh, Anna!'

She's going mad again. Maybe it's a hypnogogic hallucination – she sometimes hears her name being called when she is just falling asleep. James has assured her this is a normal phenomenon. But she's not falling asleep now. It's her gym instructor's voice. She turns towards the voice and sees her picking up a packet of frozen raspberries from the freezer section. It must be her lunch break.

'I saw you.'
'It's not for me, it's for a friend.'
The instructor gives her a look that says she doesn't believe her. Wanting to avoid any more altercations, she goes the long way around the aisles, cutting through the back to reach the checkout. This will be her last, short-lived attempt at the gym. It is far too stressful and demoralising in every way. She'll have to stick to walking around the block a few times instead. Besides, she can now navigate the block by herself and not experience the lost at sea feeling she'd previously experienced on her release from hospital. When she turns up for the movie night and tells her

friends about the encounter, Anne laughs and says: 'Remember the time when we went shopping for my party and loaded the whole confectionery aisle into the trolley? They gave us a look at the counter as though we were sugar addicts.'

She wishes she could remember this but it's like trying to see through scratched glass. Even with the glass removed, she is dubious there will be any memory behind it. Small events and memories have been taken from her; moments whisked away. Photographs, writing, and things people say jolt and surprise her, making her feel uncomfortable about her memory. She feels like she's finger-painting in a child's version of a picture when the real memory had previously existed in realistic oils. It makes her feel wary at what else has been taken. She begins to feel like a dementia patient in a nursing home: that feeling of not being able to access your own memory is awful. Now she gets a glimpse of how Grandad might feel. She knows she cannot write about memory without mentioning her grandfather.

Cardea \ Herringbone stitch / 2012

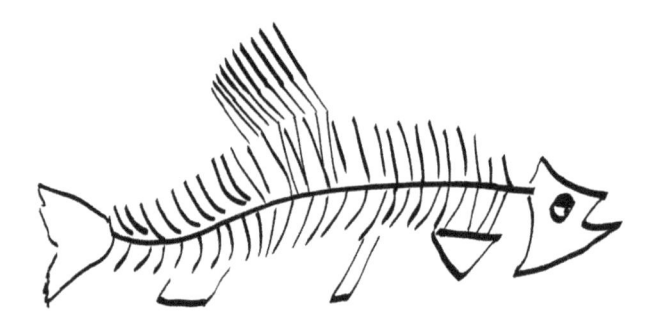

She turns the wrong way to go to Nana and Grandad's old room at the nursing home, forgetting that Grandad is in a different ward now with a single room. Like Grandad, her mind has erased the memory that Nana has passed away. Mum reminds her it's the other way and they discover Grandad, who can't find his room either. He is wandering, lost with his wheelie walker between the fish tank and fake flowers. They walk with him back to his room. The cup of tea on his tray is still warm. Some days Grandad remembers he used to run a clothing factory, manufacturing suits and dresses. The sign still gleams in Fortitude Valley, 'Freedman and Co', gold letters on brick. At home, a green notebook 'Pocket Secretary' is filled with notes and sketches Nana drew to help Grandad with the latest women's fashions. Mum tells Grandad that he's looking good.

'You mean my clothes are clean,' he says.

Sometimes Grandad rings five times in one day, forgets the hour-long conversation and rings again ten minutes later. Today is one of those days, but this time, Mum is out.

'Hello? Hello? Is this Sari?'

'Hi Grandad – no, it's Anna, Sari's daughter, your granddaughter.'

'Oh. So, you're not Sari?'

'No, I'm Anna. Mum's out but you can talk to me.'

'It's a funny thing but something's happened to my memory. I don't know where I am. I seem to be in a hotel.'

No doubt the vases of dry flowers are confusing for Grandad as his mind tries to assemble meaning from the unfamiliar things around him.

'Don't worry, Grandad, I know – it looks a bit like a hotel, but you're in a nursing home.'

'I can't find my wallet to pay for all this.'

'It's all paid for. You don't have to worry.'

'I don't know where I am.'

'There should be a button you can press to get a nurse.'

'A button? I can't see a button.'

'Or if you go just outside your door there are nurses who can help.'

'Where's Adele?'

The question punches her in the guts, and she knows what's coming.

'She's – passed away.'

'What? No one told me. My darling Adele. I need to call people to let them know, we need to organise the funeral. How did this happen? How could I have forgotten something like this?'

'It happened two years ago now.'

'Two years ago!'

'There was nothing more you could have done. You were there by her side in the ambulance. You were there at the funeral.'

'I don't know how I could forget a thing like that. How on earth could I forget that? My memory.'

These are the most emotional kinds of conversations, when he relives the tragedy of her passing over again as though for the first time.

'There's a book we put together for you. It has pictures of you and the family and tells you about your life and what happened to Nana. It's in the top drawer.'

'Ah yes, I can see something here.'

'Your door is the closest one to the dining room and nurses' station, so if you just walk outside, one of the nurses will be able to help you.'

'You're sure?'

'Yes. But I can ring the nurses' station and get them for you – would you prefer that? I'd just have to hang up the phone to ring them. Would that be okay?'

'I feel lost.'

'Don't worry, Grandad – we know where you are. We'll be visiting on the weekend.'

'But how will you know where I am? I don't even know where I am.'

'We'll find you. I promise.'

On her next visit with Mum, Dad, and Alan, Grandad is in fine form with his sayings.

'I'm away with the fairies. That's something you say when it's your birthday because there are fairies dancing on the cake. I remember.'

'Try drinking some of your tea,' says Mum.

'If I reach zero, I get a prize,' he says.

She loves the lines he comes up with. They sound profound.

Grandad remembers who Mum is, but he can't seem to place her. She blames her hospitalisation, when she'd been absent for months. Maybe because she hasn't been able to visit as frequently, his mind had forgotten her. It's different to when he doesn't remember her voice in phone conversations. When she visits in person and he stares through her, it's as devastating as if she's lost a grandparent.

Grandad goes through stages of wanting to run away from the nursing home, of planning to escape with his friendly maxi taxi driver, who once took Nana everywhere in the wheelchair. He is agitated about his memory and cannot remember where he is. He rings and forgets. Rings and forgets. When he forgets how to use the phone altogether, they wish for the times he would ring and be able to remember them and talk. At their next visit, she and Grandad sit outside while Mum talks to one of the nurses and Dad gets the tea. A bruise blooms along his thumb, the colour of old blood. Fumbling with the chocolate wrapper, he says, 'I can't seem to open this wrapper. Can you do it?' She opens the wrapper and he eats the chocolate in one go. She plucks some grapes for him and lets him know that they're washed, but he is distracted.

'There's something on the road. I think it's an animal. A dog,' he says.

She scans for signs of roadkill.

'There's nothing there, Grandad. Just the shadows.'

But he's unsettled now; she can tell by the way his eyes close and the lines on his forehead crease. He gazes intently at the road as cars race one after the other over shadows that look like dead dogs. She wheels him inside and sits on the familiar red-and-black checked blanket. Reaching into the top drawer for his memory book, she brings out the words and photographs she helped compile that tell him about his life, his children, his grandchildren.

'Who's that?' he says and points to a picture.

'That's you,' she says.

He gives her a smile that's also filled with mischief. Only they are in on the joke. And for a moment it's just like old times. He turns and gazes at her and for a moment she thinks he really sees her. Then he looks at the bowl in her hands and frowns.

'Grapes,' he says. 'Are they washed?'

Each visit is different and she never knows what version of Grandad she'll get. Today he smiles when they all wave at him.

'Some of the family is in Italy,' says Mum, giving a family update of their aunt's and uncle's whereabouts. 'They went to see the Statue of David.'

Grandad points to Dad.

'Not my David,' she laughs. Afterwards they will talk in excitement about how he remembered Dad's name.

Today he doesn't touch the apples and instead has cravings for bananas. Mum brings out two. He turns to Alan and says, 'I gave you permission to grow that beard', then calls him by his name. She opens the lid to her banana caramel cake, wondering if her turn for the remembered naming will come too. Grandad says, 'here's to the cake maker'. He looks at her and she looks back. Then he says, 'where's your beard?' They laugh at his joke. She's no longer just the photo taker, the memory catcher, the listener. Today she's the cake maker, whose name is still lost, but it's a start.

She begins to get used to this other version of Grandad. Grandad is always pleased to see them, even if he can't quite place them, and he still has his own quirks. He loves the different food they bring – a welcome change from the nursing home staples. She often makes Nana's recipes as though they are magic spells to ignite memory. After baking a honey cake for Rosh Hashanah, when they arrive at the nursing home, she watches eagerly as he eats a piece, and he catches her looking.

'Don't watch, cake maker,' he says, mouth full.

When Passover comes around, she opens Nana's recipe book, finds the Passover fruitcake recipe. She soaks mixed fruit in a bowl with a Kiddush cup of sweet kosher wine. She creams butter and sugar, adds six eggs one by one. In goes almond and matzo meal with a teaspoon of cinnamon. They arrive at the nursing home for second night Seder and Grandad recognises the box of matzah. Says 'Pesach!' with an incredulous expression as though wondering how he could forget.

He sings along to the Ma Nishtana in Hebrew, and though his voice is soft she sneaks glimpses of him mouthing the words. He reaches a hand to his head, making sure his yarmulke is still in place. As he raises his wine cup for Kiddush, his hand is steady. He eats some matzah with maror. Mum asks if he would like some gefilte fish or herring. Throughout the meal his right hand holds the base of the Kiddush cup, the touch familiar. He is offered a pickle.

'Should be safe,' he says.

She passes him a piece of Passover fruitcake. She waits, hopeful that Nana's recipe will kindle taste-memory. That he will recall a sweetness only this cake can bring. He takes a bite, and she waits for his response. She is disappointed when there is only worry over crumbs. But as her uncle wheels him back to his room, Grandad notices the photo of Nana on the wall, and says, 'That's my darling wife.'

She wishes someone would bake a memory cake for her.

She needs all the clues and prompts she can get. And she knows where the biggest one lurks – her hospital file. She just doesn't know how to gain access to it.

Cardea \ Zigzag stitch / 2012

She still needs clues to her own story. She wants to know what happened to her in hospital in 2011. Somewhere in dungeon depths, her file hides in a manila folder. At her next appointment, she asks James how to go about obtaining a copy.

'I think it's a good idea if patients read their own file, to understand. You should be able to access it under the Freedom of Information Act. Have a look online on the hospital website.'

She looks up the website at home and follows the instructions to apply. She rings the number provided, to find out how long it will take to receive a copy.

'About six to eight weeks if the file is quite large. You'll receive all the information on a CD,' says the voice on the end of the line.

She recalls the size of her file, which James writes in each visit: thicker than a novel. It would take a while to scan. She tries to distract herself while waiting.

She's walking through the State Library of Queensland when she sees a flyer listing 'what's on' at the Queensland Writers Centre. Coming up are a series of poetry workshops called *Unlocking Your Poetic Voice 2012* run by Pascalle Burton. She vividly remembers seeing Pascalle perform while working as a volunteer at the Brisbane Writers Festival, back when she'd been studying photography. Pascalle's performance had combined music, visuals, and poetry and she'd been inspired by this woman with long red hair. Now, five years later, she decides to sign up to her classes straight away.

At their first class, Pascalle brings out some books and magazines with graphics and photographs for the poets to use as leaping points for their writing. In one class they learn about the sound of words through assonance and consonance and inner rhyme. She's never heard of assonance before – the repetition of the vowel sound to create internal rhyming, and consonance – repetition of the same consonant. She realises she needs to pay attention to the sounds of words themselves and that there is so much to consider when writing a poem. In the break, Pascalle brings out some brownies with macadamia nuts and raisins that she's baked for them. Towards the end of the course, Pascalle says it's important to have goals as a poet and that these goals don't necessarily have to be winning the Thomas Shapcott at the Queensland Poetry Festival. Her ears prick up: the elusive Thomas Shapcott Prize for an unpublished manuscript. Now that she's survived psychosis, and poetry has taken over as her new form of expression, her dream is to make the shortlist.

The eight weeks of waiting for her file pass. Each day she checks the letterbox, returning disappointed. When her phone rings, she tries not to sound too dejected.

'Hi, I'm calling about your request for a copy of your file, which was to be due this week. Because of the sheer volume of your file, we're asking your permission for a two-week extension so we can keep working on it.'

Her spirits lift that they haven't forgotten her.

'It's for you,' says Mum.

She can tell from her mother's voice that it's from the hospital. She takes the envelope but it's not thick enough to contain a copy of her file and she can't feel the imprint of a CD inside.

> I refer to your recent application ... access to the 524 pages is refused ... I have examined the record and I am concerned that the record contains material, which could cause you some concern and could be prejudicial to your physical or mental health and wellbeing ...

> I have decided that access should be given instead to your treating health care professional ... please contact the office to provide contact details of the healthcare professional ... if you do not provide the information to this office by the date below, I will close my file on this matter.

She sits in the chair opposite James and hands him the letter of refusal. He gives it his full attention, staring intently at the wording. It's her only clue left. It's her information. They can't keep it from her. Their refusal just makes her want to read it more. As though they're hiding something from her. Her nails dig into the skin of her hands while she waits for James's response.

'I believe patients should be given access to their files should they request it. Once I receive your file on CD, I'm happy to go through it with you and then give you the CD, so you can look at it over the week and come back. We can then discuss any concerns or questions you may have. How does that sound?'

She nods, grateful as always she has James as her psychiatrist.

A third of the year has now passed since she initially requested her file. James scrolls down the 500-page document and she glimpses many different types of scrawled handwriting from nurses. She had thought everything would be typed. Graphs and test results spin down.

'Here, bring your chair closer so you can see.'
She brings her chair across, text imprinting on her brain:

No coherent speech on response to questions – asks upon greeting if the doctor can cut her hair. Plan: admit to seclusion, too agitated to manage.

Patient unable to recall if she 'did a photography degree or was in hospital'. Doctor contacted parents who confirmed that she has an Honours degree in photography.

At home, she makes herself a strong cup of tea and begins to read the file, typing fragments into her diary, transcribing so she won't have to go back to scrutinise the handwriting again later.

She goes through slowly, methodically, unpicking each word and making notes like a detective. The work is emotionally draining but she types with detachment because it's not the 'real her' she's reading about – it's another 'her' from an alternate universe. It's a monkey in a cage, pouring yoghurt on its head. She watches this figure from a distance as it screams in seclusion. There's a bomb in the locked drawer about to explode. The figure smashes fire alarms, tells a nurse that she fears someone is going to chop off her head and one hand. This creature believes she is in an ant farm; that she has gone back to kindergarten. She types and types and types. She asks if she has a twin. Wants a CCTV camera. Believes she is pregnant. She is going to have a miscarriage in hospital. Hitler and Osama bin Laden are coming to get her. She is evil and the devil. Osama bin Laden has put a bomb in the locker; she is Osama bin Laden. She is also Hitler and in turn, Voldemort. The worst, most evil beings her mind can conjure.

It seems the news, history, and popular fiction had infiltrated her psychosis. In the file she finds the night before her first round of ECT commenced. She had thrown a bowl of soup at one of the nurses and was put in seclusion. She had smuggled in a pen, which was taken away by security. *Instead of drinking the resource, used the straw to drip the fluid as ink to write on the floor.* What she wrote on the floor was not recorded. Some of her notes make their way into found poems. She reads how she pocketed tablets in the side of her mouth, spat them out into her hand and slid the dissolving tablets into the folds of her clothing. She reads she was scared of the male nurses and kicked one in the groin. She'd tried to grab the keys from around another nurse's neck. She never knew she was capable of such things. She glimpses a picture of a clock; a circular watch face that James had drawn when he had asked her to tell him the time. This too had made it into her file, but it seems the photograph she'd seen paperclipped to her file had not. There is a page that reads: page 369 redacted for the following reason: *Contrary to Public Interest*. The entire page has been censored and she wonders what they don't want her to see. She drags herself away from the computer, her eyes prickling with tiredness. It has taken her time to detangle the handwriting and she's managed to read through the night.

Anna can't remember me.

Asked staff whether she is alive

Little response to treatment – at risk

Deranged

Very long curly hair

Continuously pressing the fire alarm

Impression: floridly psychotic. Risk: misadventure

Was only able to supply 1 drop of urine, insufficient.

Ate w/ her hands.

<u>*Thought form:*</u> *Loosening of associations and derailment were present*

<u>*Thought content:*</u> *Persecutory delusions*

Anna was threatening after ECT, holding a spoon, stating:
'Stay away from me, do not come close!'

She had forgotten.

Her mind is a whirl at her next appointment.

'Did you feel it was you when you read it?' asks James.

'No, it felt as though I was reading about someone else. It wasn't me. I mean, it was "me", but I wasn't there.'

'Did it make you feel sad?'

'Sad for the person who went through it,' she says.

She feels nothing she says makes sense, even though they're the truest words she can find.

'So now that you've read it, how do you feel?'

'I'm glad to know what was on my file.'

'Is there anything else you want to ask me?'

She thinks of what Stephanie-the-case-manager had written about her. She hadn't realised the notes from her visits would be included in her file. She knew her notes wouldn't be flattering but she wasn't prepared for the adjectives she'd used to describe her. Now she realised how twisted Stephanie's view of her had been. She'd written that she was 'unkempt' and 'dishevelled' in her notes. She wants to say something to James about her notes and challenge them in some way but pushes this aside and focuses on more important matters. She asks: 'Why was a page removed?'

He frowns. 'What page?'

'369,' she says, remembering the redacted notification.

He flips through her file and finds the page, his fingers drumming the desk.

'I think there was a mix-up and another patient's information had accidentally slipped into your file by mistake.'

She's relieved that's all it is, but still feels concerned things have been censored from her. The words used to describe her echo in her head.

frizzy   distressed   poor judgement

fearful   insight nil

dysphoric   anxious   perplexed

vague   fatuous smile

when encouraged to talk normally, patient laughs

some word finding difficulty

'You were in seclusion many times. More than most people. Do you remember this?' James's face is concerned.

'No, I don't remember.'

She does not remember her seclusions, but Mum does. On one visit, no one appeared to be supervising the seclusion room. The door was slightly ajar. Her mother stepped inside. She saw her lying on a bare mattress on a cold cement floor. Mum will later tell her that seeing her in seclusion was the hardest and most emotional of times. After the session with James, she recognises the occupational therapist from her old ward in the corridor. He hands her a pottery heart from an A4 envelope. The pottery is glazed indigo and white, still warm from the oven. At home she places the heart on her windowsill.

Alan is studying to be a personal trainer and keeps encouraging her to get out of the house and to walk up Mount Coot-tha with him. Sometimes she imagines what would have happened had no one been awake at midnight to stop her from climbing Mount Coot-tha, the night of her madness. She pictures SES volunteers scouring the mountain dressed in orange, calling her name. She imagines mud smeared across her face – a hidden troll under the wooden butterfly bridge. She is fearful that walking through the mountain paths now might erupt something in her mind and propel her into the grips of psychosis for a second time. It's a shame because she misses the mountain and once felt peaceful and at home on its tracks. She has a memory of waking at 5 o'clock on a foggy morning, dragging herself out the door and photographing lacy spider webs caught between ghostly branches until the sun glowed gold through mist. She'd used the Yashica medium format film camera she'd found at a second-hand camera fair, because the world looked magical through its ground glass viewfinder. Now on those early rare foggy mornings, she turns over and goes back to sleep, not wanting to tempt fate.

But Alan's personal training mission statement echoes in her mind: *my outdoor personal and group training will rid you of stress and anxiety and stop fear from ruling your life.* She puts on her shoes. Walking up the footpath adjacent to the forest, she feels surreal. She is aware of her heart in her chest. But she goes with it. She crosses the road and stands at the green 'Mount Coot-tha Forest' sign, etched with a feathery owl. Alan walks beside her at the start and then, once he sees she's okay, picks up the pace and walks ahead on the track. Other walkers appear out of the forest as suddenly as scrub turkeys dashing across the path. Only the quick scuff of dirt and crunching of stones is the giveaway that they are coming around the bend. They pass and the bush swallows them up.

It's the scent of the forest that makes her feel like she is returning home. Something about the ochre dirt of the track and the trees. The air feels better here. The 'return to place' had evoked the feelings from her 'before' self, and not from the self that was unwell. She knows this is a good thing. They reach the first seat, her pulse beating in her ears. She doesn't know how she could have stayed away for so long. There is nothing to fear here. Being out in the world again is what she needs.

'Thanks for the walk, bro. I think I'm done for today.'

'Just a bit further. You have to see the view. It's nearly sunset.'

As she rounds the bend, the landscape opens out over the water tower and a flock of cockatoos take off into the pink-orange sky.

'Amazing?'

'Yeah.'

They run laughing through the bush, slapping at midges, trying to beat the falling darkness on their way back home. She knows then that things between her and the mountain will be okay. She no longer fears the landscape for calling her when she was at her most ill. Mount Coot-tha is once again a place where she can escape to feel better. She feels that part of the world she connected to, which had been cordoned off to her, has reopened again.

A year has passed since her madness – her Involuntary Treatment Order has finally been revoked, which also means that soon she will no longer have access to James through the public health system. She will have to find another psychiatrist. His private practice is also on the other side of town and his patient list is full. As a favour to James for his support over the past year, and for his kindness and understanding, she has agreed to participate in an interview to help his Early Psychosis Team and their research. He has promised her that the interviewer will treat her with respect.

The interviewer who visits her home promises to lock the audio file in a safe at the hospital. They sit together outside on the patio for privacy. The researcher's hair is immaculate. The woman taps the red record button on her phone.

On her last visit to James, he shakes her hand just as he had when she'd first met him. He wishes her well and she tells James something she can finally put words to from the past few weeks: 'I feel like I'm back in my own body now.'

'I often hear that from patients who have experienced psychosis. It's a good sign.'

She will miss James, but not the hospital where her appointments have taken place. As she leaves, she hopes the doors sliding closed behind her will do so for the last time. She knows that while every camera may monitor her on the way out, the cameras can't see her transformation, this subtle shift in embodiment. Cardea is no longer. Anna is back.

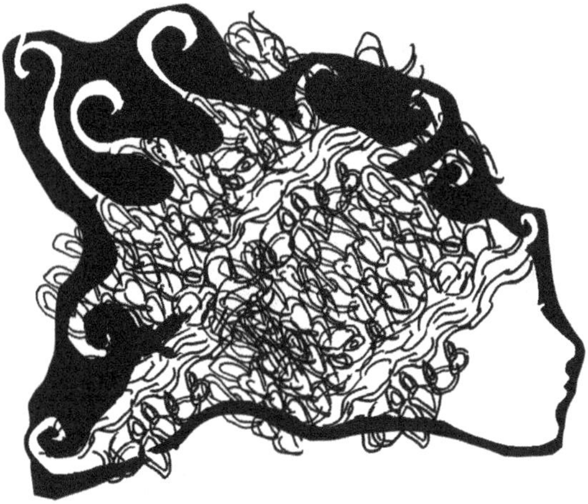

After \ Owning your knitting / 2013–2016

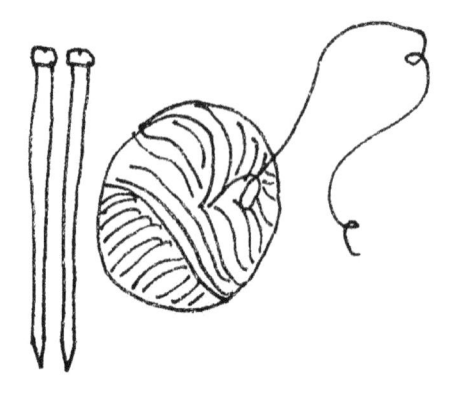

The psychiatrist I have been seeing since James, Patrice, has long hair and seems to care. We are often interrupted by at least one phone call from her mobile, which sits on the desk. But if I ever need to get in touch about a symptom, she replies to my email or phone call quite quickly. She has dark circles under her eyes, which sometimes look permanently bruised by tiredness. Sometimes she tells me I am her most creative patient. One year after starting with Patrice, I ask about coming off my medication – specifically the antipsychotic. James had told me that I'd need to stay on an antipsychotic for one to two years but could consider coming off it after that. My meds have not only caused me to put on over fifteen kilograms, but they make me sedated – a zombie.

'I don't want a repeat of what happened at hospital,' she says.

I am shut down and silenced. My views on the matter are swept away as absurd in one minute and not discussed further. I am shocked at the change in her character the minute I try to show agency for how I would prefer my treatment to go. I escape the sterile office feeling deflated and confused. The only way to shake off these kinds of visits is by seeing friends and family.

I remember visiting Grandma soon after I got out of hospital. Dad drove us to Grandma's place in Southport with its pawpaw tree out the front and mango tree out the back. On that visit I found out she spoke up to eight different languages: English, French, Hungarian, and a smattering of Italian, Russian, Polish, and Yiddish. She told me she could swear in Arabic. Her family was Hungarian. She was born in Egypt and lived there until she was eleven. Her family was expelled and fled to Italy for six months in a refugee camp, trading bread to survive, before moving to Australia. She met her husband when she was fifteen-and-a-half – became engaged at seventeen, had my father at nineteen. That visit, Dad told her I'd been unwell, but hadn't mentioned the psychosis. Grandma had recommended drinking mulled wine with cloves and she passed me an orange.

'Here darlink, take it.'

Today, Grandma tells us her freezer has stopped working. We ask what she did with the chicken, and she says she fed it to the fishes. She serves us orange cake.

'The oranges are boiled with their skins on,' she says.

Since the chemo treatments, her hair now curls – bright white. She gives us a pineapple top and says – 'plant the top of this pineapple and another will grow.'

Celery grows in a margarine tub filled with water on her windowsill. She explains how it regrows – my brother takes up the challenge at home. By the time Grandma's in hospital, our celery is shrivelling up. Dad asks a nurse if the woman on the hospital bed is his mother. Her strong and fierce self so changed. On the way back to Brisbane we pick up pies for dinner and dessert from Yatala. Each trip to the hospital results in a pie. By the fourth week we can't eat another one.

A pottery cup fills with used teabags – strings trail out like fair rides gone wrong. It stands as an offering. I consider photographing it – calling it *the day grandma dies*. I can't bring myself to do it, write a poem instead. At the funeral, the rabbi cuts my father's shirt with scissors – Kriah. In Jewish funeral custom, immediate family tear their own clothes for a loved one who has died. Afterwards we search Southport for cups of tea. My father's hands are muddy from shovelling dirt, torn shirt obvious beneath his tie. We go to synagogue on Friday night. My father says Kaddish for Grandma. Afterwards we order Chinese takeaway, stand in a tight-knit group, facing each other, talking softly, waiting for our name to be called. Grandma had once told me she'd been an extra in a movie in the '90s. I'd never found out which one. Maybe I would watch every single '90s film, just for a glimpse of Grandma somewhere in the background, eyes trained not on the lead actors, but the crowds.

I am travelling around Perth with two of my friends, Anne and Hui. We are on a road trip, talking about the last time we'd been there three years earlier in 2010. I can't remember anything from our trip – it had been the year before my madness and I know we went, just not the details, especially not the wineries we had visited or the beautiful scene of flowers we had stumbled across that Anne is talking about.

'I can't believe you don't remember?'

I've crossed the line between vague and forgetful.

When I was released from hospital in 2011, doctors advised me not to tell my friends about my psychosis and hospitalisation. But now, years on, I decide to finally tell them.

'You know how I wasn't well years ago and kind of disappeared for a bit?'

'Yeah.'

'Well, I was in a psychiatric hospital and had psychosis and that combined with ECT affected my memory.'

I look at the floor of the car feeling sandpaper raw, adding: 'Don't worry, I won't suddenly go mad.'

'I wasn't worried about that, Anna! I was just thinking how much you've been through,' says Anne.

Telling my friends is a huge step for me in acknowledging and sharing this part of my identity.

At my next appointment with Patrice, her eyes seem distracted by my feet for many minutes before she asks: 'Have you had your pinky toes amputated?' I am wearing sandals to the session. I explain that my smallest toes naturally curl under my other toes and feel too self-conscious to wear sandals to any future sessions. She asks me about my anxiety and recommends a psychologist she thinks will be a good fit for me – Wembley.

When I arrive for my appointment with Wembley there is a smell in the room: a really farty smell. I must have farted and not realised. I can't keep track of all the questions because I'm so worried about the farty smell. After three or so minutes Wembley says: 'I should probably tell you at this point that the air conditioner is releasing some pretty noxious gases. I thought it important I flag this with you, just so you know it's not me.'

He says he has to write down the exact time that it happens so the air con can be fixed properly. He holds up a post-it note with several times written down as evidence. I start to wonder if these weird situations only happen to me.

Next time I go to my appointment, the same farty smell emanates from the air con and at the end of my session, when the receptionist asks what time I would prefer, I decide to give the 2 o'clock time slot a miss and try for the morning. I discover it is less smelly then.

The more I go to my psychology sessions, the less sure I am he can help with my anxiety.

'Now, let me explain this graph to you,' he says, heading over to the whiteboard.

Anxiety,
    triggers,
        exposure,
learning memory,
  time,
subjective units of distress,
    social situation,
        avoidance,
          0 to 100

'So, your homework is to notice what you think others think of you.'

'Why would I want to notice what I think others think of me?'

'We need to find out what your internal self-image is.'

I pause and say, 'I don't want to think what I think others think of me.'

'That's the most insightful thing you've said today.'
'But—'
'Let me explain—'

Allocation of attention / important
        self-directed / external cues /
                can't concentrate on the / situation.

Wembley loves his graphs. I do not like graphs.

Next, he asks me to stare at the pot plant on his side table. He asks me to notice the colour of the leaves, the shape of the pot, how the leaves end in a tint of white, while he says: 'Now you're probably thinking this is stupid – you're hungry or thirsty – I want you to acknowledge and accept these thoughts but then focus back on the pot plant.' I focus on the fake pot plant. I think this is ridiculous. I focus on the pot plant.

After a while I forget the point of the exercise and can only remember staring at a mass-produced plastic pot plant for many minutes. Towards my eighth session he begins to sense I am disillusioned with the whole process and asks me to be transparent with him. I say I don't like the whiteboard and I don't want him to draw graphs on it. He asks me if I like the board when it's blank. I say yes. He is taken aback. He fidgets with the whiteboard marker pen as though unsure of how to proceed. I do not return for another appointment and soon after, Wembley moves interstate.

I've been attending more poetry readings lately. David Stavanger is the Lord Mayor's Writer in Residence at the Brisbane Square Library and coordinates Couplet. He also won the 2013

Thomas Shapcott Poetry Prize for his collection *The Special*, and his poems about mental illness resonate with me. I glimpse Pascalle at one of the events. She wears an amazing glittery red brooch that has pearls as teeth, which she made herself, inspired by Salvador Dali. I say hello, admiring her brooch.

'Anna! Let me introduce you to David,' she says.

David has a tattoo of a vine, which curls up his neck and around his left ear. I've seen him perform as his alter ego Ghostboy at a SpeedPoets event and as an MC for Brotherhood of the Wordless a few years ago. As Ghostboy, he wears black lipstick, and his performances are gripping. In person, as David, he is warm and kind.

'Congratulations on winning the Thomas Shapcott,' I say.

'Thank you. You write poetry?' he says.

'Yeah.'

'That's great. I've seen you here often. Thanks for coming along.'

When I hear David is performing at Poets Up Late at the West End Library, I decide to go. On the night of the reading, the rain lashes, and storms grumble. I make it to the upstairs section of the library, where I can just see the chairs in the darkness, filled with a jumble of poets. I wonder if there's been a partial blackout.

'Would you like the lights on?' asks one of the library staff.

'No, it's great how it is. Poets prefer to read in the dark,' says David.

David goes on stage and describes himself as a poet and lapsed psychologist. He says he used to be a Special, a term he created for his book. He says: ' "To special" is to observe a suicidal or psychotic mental health in-patient overnight with limited support or sleep.' He reads poems from his collection, and I hang on to every word.

Next month at Couplet, David says he has read some of my poems. My poem 'Crunchy, No Bruises' about my grandad's memory, had recently been selected for *Rabbit: A journal for nonfiction poetry* by guest editor Felicity Plunkett. Felicity, who I greatly admire, won the Thomas Shapcott Prize in 2008 for her collection *Vanishing Point* and I have been keen to share my work with her. David said he liked the absurdity of my 'Dream Diary' poem that was selected for *Cordite*, which Felicity had also coincidentally been the guest editor for. Submissions for *Cordite* are judged without the poets' names, which are only revealed to the editors after they make their choices. These were the first two of my poems that had ever been accepted by publications that paid for poetry. Felicity had sent me an encouraging message afterwards:

> I've really enjoyed reading your sparky, unique work recently. As you probably know, the odds for selection for *Cordite* were pretty dire – only 40 out of a submitted 1500 poems could be published, so there were more I'd like to have selected, and I really love the ones I did select.

She encourages me to enter the Thomas Shapcott Prize. I print out her lovely email and blu-tack it to the door of my study. The next month, I click open David's message inviting me to feature at Couplet at the Brisbane Square Library. It's a paid fifteen-minute set. I feel both surprised and honoured. I never thought I'd be able to perform my poems because of my anxiety. But I say yes, choose and order my poems, and practise. The night of my first reading arrives, and Dad records the event on his phone. The applause after David announces me follows like a wave pushing me onwards to the microphone. I am wearing one of Nana's outfits from when she was younger – her long emerald dress. A red silk flower is pinned in my hair. I'm aware my legs are shaking and hope the dress hides the tremors. A large crowd fills the library space with my family and friends and other poetry lovers. Their warm response strengthens my resolve after each poem.

Afterwards, the poets and I head to The Fox, and I find myself at the end of a long table at the bar, sitting next to David. I tell him how much I connect with his poetry. A noisy bar probably isn't the best place to shout about how I was hospitalised with psychosis, but when the other poets go around the corner for a smoke, I pick a quiet moment to tell him. He listens to my story and understands. I still haven't shared my experiences with many people who are not my immediate family, or a doctor. After this first poetry reading, my confidence begins to come back.

Soon I am preparing the final order and tweaks for my manuscript for the 2015 Thomas Shapcott Poetry Prize. I feel it's the first time all my poems flow and fit together since I first began entering the prize in 2012 and I'm proud of this manuscript – it's built on four years' work. I print off the copies, and then head to the post office to send it to the Queensland Poetry Festival. Mid-August arrives, the time when winners and shortlisted entrants are due to be emailed about the results of the Thomas Shapcott Prize. I check my email every hour but don't hear anything. I assume I haven't made the shortlist this time round. Two days before the festival, my heart skips a beat when I read the email heading *Confidential: Thomas Shapcott Prize 2015*. I click it open and read:

Dear Anna

We are writing to inform you that your poetry manuscript was short-listed for the 2015 Arts Queensland Thomas Shapcott Prize. **Please keep this email in confidence as the results of all the prizes are embargoed until their announcement at QPF's One Crowded Hour Fri 28th August at Judith Wright Centre 6–7pm.** This year's winner has also been contacted and will be announced at this event.

'Mum! Dad! I've been shortlisted for the Thomas Shapcott Poetry Prize!'

'That's wonderful, darling, congratulations.'

'I haven't won – it says the winner has already been contacted, but it's still a really big deal. Lots of poets who have been short-listed for the prize have been able to get their manuscripts published with other publishers too.'

I read further down the email and see I'm invited to attend a masterclass with Felicity Plunkett and previously shortlisted entrants and poets 'identified by the judges as having a poetic voice or talent that is deserving of further support and development'. I feel honoured to meet the editor who selected my first poems and supported me, and she is every bit as kind in person as in email correspondence.

A few months before I graduate from my creative writing degree in 2015, I have a consultation with my tutor. This semester I have written poetry about the women in my family – the matriarchs. As the consultation ends and my tutor picks up his leather satchel to leave, I pause and ask: 'What are your thoughts about publishing poems or stories about mental illness?'

He puts his satchel down again. Even though I've kept my experience with memory loss and psychosis quiet throughout uni, I tell him a bit about it. How I'd had no agency or self for two months as an involuntary patient in 2011. He is understanding and says that it's up to the person when to put it out there. We discuss women's treatment in psychiatric hospitals, and he encourages me to think about doing a PhD. Then he says: 'You want to own it.'

I graduate from my creative writing course with distinction. As I shake the chancellor's hand he says, 'we're so proud of you'. Only I can hear what he says, above the claps and cheers from my family and friends. And for a moment I wonder if he knows about the psychosis. I wonder if he senses what this achievement means for me and if he knows that I sometimes look over my shoulder, watching for the psychosis beast, my foe; that I am now kitted out for my mission with more understanding and awareness. When I sit down with my degree in hand in the stands, I lip-read what the chancellor says to the next person, curious. I see him say the words: 'We are so proud of you', and I am glad.

Before I lose access to the university database, I search for papers written on psychosis in the library search engine. The database comes up with a study completed in South East Queensland. I click on it, knowing that I had been one of the participants. I realise that the paper has only just been published, four years later. The study I was in, 'The prevalence and correlates of childhood trauma in patients with early psychosis', found that over three-quarters of the one hundred patients who had experienced early psychosis had also been exposed to trauma.

It's now been three years since Grandma gave us the pineapple top. Today, a miniature pineapple has appeared. Perfect as thumbprint whorls. I realise I've subconsciously checked for pineapples each time I've passed the plant. I wait for it to ripen. After months, my brother picks it, cuts it in four. The pineapple is the best I've ever tasted, but saves its sourness for my father's piece. We keep the top to plant another day.

I decide to start writing my memoir after seeing the Year of the Memoir course advertised with the Queensland Writers Centre. I see that Kári Gíslason, author of *The Promise of Iceland*, will run the course all day once a month for five workshops. The course will start in February 2016. I'd had Kári as a lecturer at uni and was inspired by his lectures. I remember one time when I was an hour early as usual due to my anxiety about being late. I was sitting outside the lecture theatre and before I knew it, Kári had turned up and sat down next to me on the floor. He was wearing sandals though it was winter and started chatting about the book we were to read that week. He asked me what I'd thought of the reading. I'd hoped to say something profound but I had struggled with it, as I was still attending Mind Gym at the time and getting back my reading concentration. But I did remember one of the characters, who we discussed in detail before it was time to head in for the lecture.

    I talk with Mum about the idea of me writing a memoir – we are standing by the pool. She is watering the bird of paradise in the garden, and I am walking along the brickwork around the edge of the pool like it's a tightrope. I feel it's important I ask if it's okay with her that I write about my experiences, as this would mean writing about the family. Mum laughs and says the difficulty is that we are such a private family but she understands my need to express myself through writing. The words begin to flow and don't stop. I also compile all the memoir material I already have and realise I've been writing short stories in the third person and novellas and poems about my experience all along. Small moments that would have otherwise escaped in that time of forgetting are all there in my writing, sometimes under the mask of other characters. I sit at the computer for eight days straight, untangling the characters and conversations and going back over diary entries. The writing gives me an energy that conquers the sedating side effects from the meds, and I get up early in the morning to write and compile. By the end of the eight days, I have the bulk of a draft to work with. Over the next seven years I will attend memoir masterclasses to hone my craft.

In the first session of the Year of the Memoir, as a way of introducing ourselves, Kári asks us to share what our memoir is about. We sit around tables in a semi-circle, and I am sitting at the end towards the door, so I can escape if needed. This means I will be going second last. Everyone has their own amazing stories to share, including another person who has had psychosis but remembers their experience in detail. It makes me feel better talking about my own story. It is a strange feeling telling the class of sixteen people, who I don't yet know, about how I woke up as though from a coma in hospital, with no memories. At the same time, it feels like a release. Everyone in the memoir course is supportive and interested.

'I sense big things for you,' one of the participants says on the last day of the course.

After I begin to compile and write my memoir, I start having recurring dreams I am wearing my old scoliosis back brace on the outside of my clothing, exposed for all to see. But in each dream, people are unfazed by the brace and this reaction reassures me. By the end of the dream it has fallen off me, left in whatever environment I have dreamt. It's in the past and I know the dream is not just about the brace, but about revealing my mad-self to others.

The Scribe Nonfiction prize opens for writers under 30. As I am now 28, I decide to submit. I've heard about the prize in the past but haven't been ready to share my experiences. I return to the first part of my manuscript and condense it into 10 000 words of power, so that it also works as a stand-alone piece. On the day that those on the shortlist will be notified, I check my computer every few minutes for an email. I am hopeful but the announcement time comes and goes. I can only sleep for four hours that night and have a nap at midday the next day. And when I wake up there it is. An email titled 'Congratulations Scribe 2016 shortlist'. The shortlisted entrants are invited to attend a masterclass in Melbourne and Scribe's 40th birthday party, where the announcement of the winner will be made. My heart beats wildly as I look up flights. This time five years ago I was coming out of a psychiatric hospital in Brisbane after my Melbourne trip. And now I will be going back to Melbourne to celebrate an extract of my memoir being shortlisted.

Mum holds my arms tight when I tell her and then she gives me a hug. I decide to book flights to Melbourne for just a few days, to dip my feet back in and see how I go. I am nervous about returning. Worried about what unexpected memories the places I see there may bring. But I've decided I'm going as an observer, so I'm distanced from it. I email Tammy, my lovely friend from my photography degree days who has since moved to Melbourne. I'd told Tammy about my hospitalisation when she last visited Brisbane, after we'd seen an art exhibition together at GOMA. I tell her that I will be visiting Melbourne and plan to stay at a hotel on Lygon Street, near the workshop. She invites me to stay at her place in Coburg instead and I say yes, getting excited about the trip.

Meanwhile, Express Media sends me the interview questions that all shortlisted entrants are to answer and fill out. In the interview are the words 'Tell us a bit about your submission to the Scribe Prize'. I decide that this is the time to reveal what happened to me – my first 'coming out' to the world about my madness. For me this is a big deal. But I feel I am ready. Also among the written interview topics is the question 'Why do you write nonfiction?'

My reasons for writing are still the same as those I wrote in the first ever homework exercise set in the first year of my creative writing degree. It was a response to the words: *Why I write*.

> I write to make sense of the world, to share my experience out of the chaos. To document characters I observe and create new ones. I write to construct magical realms that I can disappear into for days at a time. Dancing through familiar yet surreal worlds.
>
> I write to become the detective, be the hero and be the villain. I write to run down hidden pathways, to explore

buildings and discover their secrets. I write as an excuse to venture into the basement of the Old Museum Building and find broken pianos lurking under staircases, brimming with story.

I write to get through difficult situations, store the material for later and then unleash it. I write to have a voice. I write because my fingers itch if I can't document something straight away. I write to create: to express, to learn, to understand, to piece together. To gather all my notes in one place and make a story.

The night before the interview comes out, I dream I am the Kraken, a mad octopus flailing in the ocean. Gradually over the years, I have told my oldest group of friends about my madness and hospitalisation. They are understanding and this is a relief. My writing friends share the link to the interview on social media the next morning and everyone is supportive, including my family, who say how proud they are of me. The night before my flight to Melbourne arrives. I feel floaty. I set my alarm. I'm packed and as ready as I'll ever be for this trip. My friend Tammy picks me up from the airport. The shortlisted entrants are supposed to hear the outcome before the big day. I go into Tammy's study and check my phone. I see the email – *Outcome of the 2016 Scribe Nonfiction Prize*. I click on it and read, the word 'unfortunately' leaping out at me, and see that I didn't win. Tammy's marmalade cat Astro pads into my room and jumps onto my sofa bed and lets me pat him.

I tell Tammy that I didn't win but am still looking forward to celebrating tomorrow.

'Yeah, of course – I'm going to celebrate with you!'

Hanging out with Tammy and another shortlisted writer, Katerina Bryant, who I become friends with at the announcement party, is special. Although my Melbourne experiences this time around are different, I don't feel ready to tackle the city and return to Caulfield just yet. I don't feel up to the unexpected memories or emotions that returning to certain places can bring. So instead, I have restful days and walk the streets of Coburg, battling through the rain to a little coffee shop where I sit and plan future writing projects.

On my last night in Melbourne the wind howls, similar to how the wind howled all those years ago when I couldn't get to sleep, in the week before my flight home. I dream of a memory machine: a theatre of shimmering wires harp-strung from stage to rafters. I feel relief and surprise that this time, memories can be recorded on a giant knitting machine; the memories knotted like bumps on a wind-up music device. When I play the memory back, it comes with music. On waking I try to remember the memory I recorded on it but all I can remember is the music it made, as though each of the strings were being strummed one by one.

After \ Social knitting / 2017–2019

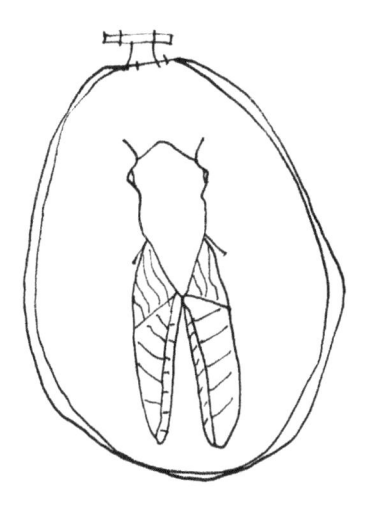

Writing is my music, my art, my power. Being creative through writing and art is how I deal with a society where I am on the margins. Poetry is my inclusive space, which is why I feel at home when the theme *Distant Voices* is announced for the 2017 Queensland Poetry Festival. I'm invited to speak on a panel about poetry and mental illness with Paula Keogh, who wrote *The Green Bell*, and Justin Heazlewood, whose book *Get Up Mum* will be published next year. David Stavanger is the chair of the session and the feeling in the room is supportive. I am wearing Nana's silk magenta and purple patterned jacket. My legs shake, even sitting down. When it's my turn to speak, I talk about moving to Melbourne in 2011 and becoming unwell. Of waking up in hospital after many rounds of ECT with no memory of my admission or hospital stay. I speak of my split selves, how I now had a part one and part two self – Before and After. How

I'd pieced myself back together with writing, poetry, and diary entries. How when I started writing, I'd discovered the process reclaims agency and my experience.

I read some poems I've been working on for my Masters degree, where I've been writing about the tensions between memory, mental illness, and Jewish identity through poetry and cultural objects. Some of these poems will later end up in my poetry collection *Amnesia Findings*, which will win the Thomas Shapcott Poetry Prize for an unpublished manuscript the following year. I have entered this prize year after year since that first poetry workshop with Pascalle. Seventh time lucky.

How to Knit a Human

Loose threads replace my body.
Frays appear unseen over time.
Threads unravel – gripped and pulled
by hundreds of invisible pincers.
Now I knit myself back into a human.
It's hard work relearning the steps –
slip-stitch, drop-stitch, pick-up-stitch, loop.
I get into a rhythm. The pattern is complex –
I drop a few stitches.
The holes form gaps in my memory.

By the end of the panel, the audience has sat with us through our journeys and is warm and receptive. I feel empowered. My braid is getting stronger, my selves woven so closely together, I am nearly whole.

At the beginning of 2018, Grandad is in hospital with pneumonia and is in palliative care. When I visit, I see he's asleep and looks more like his old self – peaceful – like from the 'before' days when he had his memory. I touch his shoulder, then move to the back of the room where I take a photograph of the inscription on his Bar Mitzvah Siddur. When Grandad stirs and tries to open his eyes, Mum tells him the whole family is here. It could be any time now. Grandad doesn't want to go yet. He's already survived for a week in hospital without water or food.

Mum says she was dreaming all night that she was holding Grandad's hand and the family were all around him and Grandad said, 'I am so happy.' She came into my room at 5am to say the time had come and Grandad had passed away. I let the thoughts rise and write them down in the order they appear – this act of remembrance. At the funeral, Mum wears a piece of clothing that can be torn and cut as part of the Kriah ritual – a white shawl with tassels. I read my poem titled 'Grandad's Passover', containing the scene where I made Nana's Passover fruitcake. How I had wanted to awaken memory and how he had recognised Nana in the photograph. A couple of days later, Alan brings back a cactus that the market stall owner had said only flowers once every six months. The next day the cactus blooms orange – a sign from Grandad.

I finish my Masters as another year passes. I remember unhooking cicada shells that cling to the bark of red flowering trees, collecting the shells in my palm in my aunt's and uncle's garden as a child. Whenever I think of the cicada I think of their shells. Never the insect itself; only the memory of it. Mum and I are now over at my aunt's and uncle's house, helping with preparations for the Passover Seder. Inside their house, we stand at the sink. My aunt has bought kosher chickens – they still need plucking. She brings out a pair of tweezers. I've never plucked a chicken before.

'It's not like plucking your eyebrows, Anna. Give it a good tug,' Mum says in amusement. An image – *I'm standing in front of the bathroom mirror, plucking my eyebrows after coming home from hospital. Tweezers were not allowed on my ward.*

I continue plucking the chicken as though nothing has happened. Leaving the rest to Mum, I grate two red apples for the charoset. The secret ingredient is date syrup. A splash of kosher wine, then almond and walnut meal bind it together. My uncle slices horseradish root – a white sliver for each person. I set the table for twenty and he asks me what I've been up to lately. I say my poetry chapbook *The Last Postman* is now out in the world and that I'm working on the final proofs of my first illustrated full-length poetry collection *Amnesia Findings*. My drawing abilities, which I feel had been severely affected as a side effect from the ECT treatments, had finally returned to me – not through practise, but from time. When my publisher had asked me what colour I'd like across the front cover, I was drawn to orange but couldn't work out why. She'd shown me a pantone swatch and I'd picked a shade straightaway. Only later did I realise the orange is the same shade of body wash I first saw on waking up in hospital eight years ago in 2011.

My memories of my mad self remain as silent and pitch-black as a tear in the universe. A black hole I am constantly reknitting myself around. How does one knit around such a nebulous, constantly moving form? Would I ever remember being so deeply unwell? Unravelled and pulled so far into another realm that even the skein of yarn disappeared with it? I can't bear the thought of going through the reknitting. Once is more than enough. Slowly, I've managed to recapture the memories from the years before my unravelling, by looking at photographs and asking Mum for stories and clues. Sometimes the weave holding back my memories is tight, but other times, just as I've lost memories through dropped stitches, some strands have travelled through the gaps. My memories are hard-won.

I will discover another strand of my identity the following year. Even though I've been attending queer book events at the library, and now have two copies of *Guidebook to Queer Jewish Spirituality* – a comic by Mira Schlosberg – on my bookshelf, I've never allowed myself the thought that I might be bi. I watch as my queer poetry friends go through all the emotions as their right to marry is voted on and challenged. The poems they write during and after this time are powerful. But it's only after getting through the yes vote in 2017 that I begin to realise my own potential queerness.

I think about how I didn't take anyone to my Grade 12 formal. Some girls wanted to take other girls as their partner to the dance but weren't allowed to by the school. This only reinforced the message that queerness was unacceptable. Perhaps if we had received education about queer identities – teachers included – and perhaps if there had been no rules about who we could bring to a dance, then maybe I could have allowed myself to know my own bi identity earlier. As a teen, I had dreams in which I was in a relationship and getting married. In the dreams, I was disappointed when I realised my partner was a woman – disappointed because I knew being married to a woman didn't count, wasn't allowed, wasn't even legal. I dismissed my married-to-a-woman dreams as irrational. This was fifteen years before the yes vote. I couldn't allow being queer as a possibility for myself – society wouldn't let me. I worry about how I unknowingly erased my queer self-knowledge for thirty years. I'm still surprised that society could infiltrate my brain, suppressing a whole part of me, to the extent that only my dreaming self knew. Now a new world has opened, and I look at everything as if seeing properly for the first time. I make the decision to move out of home and into a share house with a couple of my queer poetry friends.

My hairdresser says there's a different kind of freedom from living out of home, and I finally understand what he means. The poetry bookshelf in the TV room of the share house is filled with all the literature on the topic I could ever need. I read through an anthology titled *Gay and Lesbian Poetry in Our Time*, trying to find my experience echoed back to me. When my housemates join me in the TV room, I hear myself say 'I think I'm coming late to the queer party'. I'm surprised the words come out, and how easy and hard it is to say them. They tell me it's not about coming late to the queer party – that there was probably a lot going on for me previously, and it wasn't the right time to realise before now – it's about subconsciously knowing when it's safe to know; that there's no instruction manual as each person is different.

To celebrate my questioning of my sexuality and the possibility of being bi, I do what any sensible girl would do – order myself a queen-sized bed and lug the bedding all the way home on the bus. My new bed is luxurious. I am unable to sleep. Previously, my sessions every two weeks with Patrice have been about her checking in on my mental state. Was I hearing voices? How was my mood on a scale of 1–10? Was I being social enough? When I talk about the possibility of being queer to Patrice, she flips through her notes and says, 'This isn't something we've talked about before.'

But it's clear Patrice is out of her depth and all she can do is advise me not to rush into sex and to not tell my family about being queer until I've sorted things out in my own head.

'Give it six months,' she says.

I ignore her advice about telling my family. Mum, Dad, and Alan are characteristically accepting and not without their humour. That night, instead of craving Magnums my family is curious to try out Golden Gaytimes.

'You know, I don't think I've ever had a Golden Gaytime,' says Mum.

We lounge around the family room; no one can be bothered walking to the corner store to buy them. Back at the share house my sleep returns. Not even the cicadas singing in summer can keep me awake at night.

I live in the poetry house for one whole year before my anxiety morphs again. It's a couple of months before my book launch. I am unable to leave my room or walk to the grocery store down the street. I decide to book into an anxiety day patient program. The course runs for one month and means I will be spending two days a week educating myself about anxiety and then putting into practice what I learn. But I get a call from the private hospital to say the program is postponed because there aren't enough numbers. The receptionist explains that many participants are too anxious to attend the anxiety course, so the hospital needs high numbers to compensate for the dropout rate. I find myself crying and did not realise how much I had been holding onto the program as my lifeline. I realise I need the support of my family once more.

Patrice increases my antidepressant dosage. The postponement means the first week of the anxiety course will now occur four days before my book launch for *Amnesia Findings*.

I move back home with my family three weeks before my book launch. The house can sense the shift of my return. When I pour boiling water into a ceramic cup for my tea, I hear a cracking sound and heat splashes my feet. The cup is still on the laminate bench but no longer whole. It stands in two perfect halves, separate as though I've sliced through a piece of wet clay with fishing line. I show Alan.

'The house can sense your stress,' he says.

In another room, the doorknob falls off in Dad's hand.

I'm forty-five minutes early, sitting on the bench outside the private hospital. I take a deep breath and head in through the Day Programs door. The professor comes into the room with a cup of tea.

He turns to our group of women and says, 'tell me a bit about yourselves and what brought you here today.'

When my turn arrives, I say I am a writer, and would like strategies to help with author events, especially my book launch on the weekend. Most of all, I would like to manage my anxiety so I can live without such a high constant level of fear.

'What is anxiety? What does it feel like for you?'

Everyone has answers: clammy, cold in the stomach, dizzy and feeling faint. But I can't quite name what anxiety feels like for me. How do you name something that you live with every day; something that sits in the background of your brain, humming and twitching a constant thrum of doubt.

'Anna? What is anxiety? How do you know when you have it?'

I try to say what I feel but can't; my mind is blank. My throat becomes constricted and tears well at the corners of my eyes.

'What are you feeling now?'

'I get emotional. I hold my anxiety in my throat. It stops me from thinking clearly.'

When we break for morning tea a fruit platter awaits, but our group all go for the raisin toast in the tearoom bread bins. Learning about anxiety is hungry work and I find out I'm not the only one whose meds make me crave sweet carbohydrates. When we return to the room, the professor says: 'Now, you've all lost control over your anxiety symptoms – but there are things you can do. Helpful things. The starting point is you. You have to want to change in terms of your own thinking and thoughts. Less negative, more positive. The world is unpredictable, yes, but it is also full of beautiful things.'

The professor looks directly at me.

'What is your fear, Anna?'

The word falls from my mouth as though it has been waiting for me all along.

'Psychosis.'

I stare at the bright watercolour painting opposite. It's the only thing in the room I can connect to, among the whiteboard and markers, grouped tables and chairs, the plastic water jugs.

'You have had this before? How many times?'

'Once. Eight years ago.'

'What happened?'

I look down at the table and the cover of the textbook for the course.

'I – don't know. It was so severe my memories of that time were taken. I just know I woke up in hospital, was told I was having ECT and had to reassemble the pieces.'

'Anna, you can now use your experience of psychosis to help yourself.'

'How? It stole my memories – took me years to recover.'

The air conditioner thrums, and the tiny scratches in the plastic cups from long-term use in the facility are disturbing me. I can smell burnt raisin toast and hospital margarine. I try to hold myself in place with the orange watercolour circle in the framed painting. I feel my emotions close to the surface of my skin again, leaking out through my eyes.

'You need to take a leap of faith. You learned the episode was horrible. If it happens again, you can learn to deal with it. It is out of your control and for eight years it hasn't happened. Therefore, it is highly unlikely it will happen again.'

'But my memories are so important to me.'

'If your memories are so important to you, why do you continue to trash them?'

I try to make sense of his words. I haven't been knowingly 'trashing' my memories – I've been hoarding them, recording them in my diary each day, not wanting to lose them again. Then I remember reading an article about how people with anxiety have difficulty concentrating and retaining knowledge. How the anxiety pushes everything else out, including memory. My own mind is working against me again.

As Mum, Dad, and Alan get ready to go to my launch, all I can manage is a piece of challah and bowl of plain rice. My family and friends appear in the sunlit foyer of the Judith Wright

In the second week of anxiety classes, we are asked to voice our concerns about speaking and my crush says he's worried that he'll blush. The psychologist asks, 'which colour?' She fans swatches like a magician and tells us she's just visited the painting section at the hardware store to choose blush-worthy samples. Oli points to Riveting Red and turns Flaming Sunset. After class, I ask Oli if he finds driving anxiety-provoking.

'No, I love driving.'

He is surprised at the extent of my fears. For me, my anxiety means I can only now drive to two places: the local pharmacy, and the local grocery store. Everywhere else I catch public transport, adding hours onto my journeys. I no longer enjoy visits to my friends, only because my stomach is in knots thinking about the drive that I'll have to make home. Patrice has made the comment 'if you find driving stressful, why bother?' With her words, the last of my driving independence is snatched away. I have had to navigate my 'After' self from scratch, the maps I'd had in my head erased, along with my confidence. My 'Before' self could manage driving to the Cultural Centre car parks along the river at South Bank and even through the busy Brisbane city streets to my synagogue for dance classes in the hall. Now I can only manage parking in a side street near Kenmore Village where the elderly buy their groceries and get scripts filled to avoid the busy car park.

I have another poetry reading in four days' time. I tell myself if I'm going to be nervous about my reading, I may as well make it worthwhile. I invite Oli along, as I know I'll be terrified whether he is there or not. It's easier asking Oli to a poetry reading than out on a date. When I mention the reading at the end of the next anxiety class, Oli says he'd love to go – he doesn't start work until

Centre, and I start to feel better. The theatre space fills. There's a special feeling in the room. Now I'm in the space and can feel the warmth and support from so many, I know I can do this. At the microphone, my nerves leave me enough that I can make myself look up at Mum when I say, 'Thank you Mum for being my first reader and sounding board. For being my memory keeper when all seemed lost. And for helping me find my way again.' There's clapping and cheering and then the signing begins. Seeing so many people from all parts of my life is wonderful – a beautiful celebration.

After the Day Program at the hospital ends, Patrice suggests I attend a night-time social anxiety course run by a psychologist. Because I am still struggling, I decide to give it a try. When I turn up at the first group session, I discover I am the only girl in a group of five anxious guys. One of the guys is quite cute. We introduce ourselves, and I find out his name is Oli. Apart from these introductions, we all sit in silence as the psychologist tries to get us to talk. The psychologist says that she herself is anxious speaking in front of the group. This does not increase my confidence.

    After the class, the guys and I gather outside on the street. We talk more freely now in the dark than we ever could under the bright fluoro lights of the psychologist's boxy whiteboard room. Oli offers to drive me home after – I am too anxious to take up his offer. Instead, I walk the cracked pavement to the bus stop, waiting in the dark just up from the pub where people shout, spill beers, and get kicked out, making their drunken way near to where I am standing. I spend the bus ride home thinking about Oli's jawline.

later that night. He asks me which suburb I live in and if he can give me a lift home tonight. This time, I say yes to a lift.

I can read poetry to a room of fifty people and ask a guy I have a crush on along, but I can't deal with things that others find easy. Like going outside. I need to physically push myself out the door, or trick myself into going, and I am forever an hour early for fear of being late. Usually, my meds only affect my right leg, which jiggles uncontrollably if I'm nervous or stressed. Before my poetry performance I put on some red lipstick. I try not to let my hands shake. I ask for a lectern when I read, so I can rest my hands on the sides.

Pacing level two of the Brisbane Square Library, I don't venture near the wavy red couch where I will perform my work overlooking the sun setting on the city. Instead, I find myself in the Romance section with authors A–J, which reminds me to keep a lookout for Oli. I glance at the artist's work of the month, trying to distract myself with the handmade jewellery in perspex display cabinets. I'm an hour early as usual. But I have confidence in my poems – I'm reading from *Amnesia Findings* tonight. I want to share my words, I'm not anxious about that, I just want to be sure nothing goes wrong before I reach the mike.

I glance again at the crowd but can't see Oli. Maybe he is too anxious to be with the audience and is around the back, hidden. But I know he hasn't shown up. I read my poems, concentrating on the rhythm and flow of each word. It's a good reading but when I walk off stage, I try not to let my disappointment show.

At the next anxiety class, Oli sits next to me in the waiting room.

'How did it go?'

He is warm and encouraging; the corners of his eyes crinkle as he smiles.

'It went really well.'

I let the sentence hang, waiting.

'I was called into work early – couldn't believe it.'

I don't have his number yet and wonder how to get it.

In class, the psychologist asks us to speak in front of a video camera for one minute and listen to the recording. She asks the group to give feedback. When my recording is played back, Oli says I have a nice voice. Afterwards, when Oli drives me home and turns in to my street, I thank him for the lift and dare to touch his shoulder. I still don't have Oli's number, but it's the last session next week, so I decide I will bundle my courage then, ask him out and get his number when he drives me home. I plan my first ever date – we will walk along the river at South Bank on my thirty-second birthday. Maybe even catch a CityCat together along the river and stand at the bow, our hair whipping back from our faces. I was either too anxious or busy trying to knit myself back together in my early twenties to give dating a go. Now, in my early thirties, I want to try it out.

For our final anxiety session, the psychologist has warned us we will have to give a five-minute presentation on any topic to practise our public speaking. I decide I will read my poems instead. I write a message for Oli in a copy of *Amnesia Findings* and choose a brown paper bag for it to go in. I slip in a card with my number. This time, I'm two hours early. The office building locks its front doors at six on the dot, so I don't want to be late to the session. I sit at the churros café and order a hot chocolate, whiling away the time. I walk up the fire escape to slow my progress but I'm still the first in the waiting room. Soon the other four guys fill the space. Oli is late. The psychologist appears and beckons us in. I want to tell her we should wait for Oli. Then she says, 'It's just the five of you today.'

At first, I think she is mistaken, but when I walk into the room, I see there are only five places laid out, instead of six. Throughout the session I try to keep back my disappointment, the paper bag by my feet. I feel ridiculous in my dress and lipstick. I try not to let my tears leak out when I read my poems. Perhaps he knew I was going to ask him out at the last session and his anxiety had ramped. Or perhaps something terrible has happened to him and the psychologist doesn't want to tell us. At the end of the session, I hang back, waiting for the others to leave.

'Is Oli okay?'

The psychologist's eyes widen, and I don't care if she wonders why I am asking – why tears are tracking my face.

'Yes, he phoned to say he was sick and couldn't make it.'

I know 'sick' means 'anxious' but can't be sure.

'I have something to give him. I don't have his contact details.'

'If you leave the parcel with me, I could pass it on – we can't give out other patients' contact details, but he'll be coming to collect the last handouts from today's session when he's better.'

I stand still, the paper bag in my hands. I don't want to hand it over. It contains too many expectations.

'I'll let you think on it while I tidy up the room.'

Maybe Oli wasn't called into work early when I had my poetry reading that afternoon – his anxiety was probably too fierce to make it, just as it was out of control for him today. I decide to give Oli one month to pick up the parcel. If he hasn't come back by then, I'll take it home.

When I check my phone three weeks later, I see a text: 'Hi Anna, it's Oli'. He is thanking me for the beautiful gift. He says he was unwell for a while. He would like to catch up for a coffee when I am free. His text was sent fourteen minutes ago. I reply, asking if he is free to see an exhibition – one of my photographs is a finalist in a photography exhibition at South Bank. I say we could check it out and then get coffee after. I wait for his reply. An hour later, he still hasn't replied. I hope he is not having a panic attack. I hope I haven't messed things up with my text in some way. When I check my phone the next morning, Oli has replied: 'Tuesday sounds great'.

I tell Patrice about Oli, and how we met in the social anxiety class, and that a relationship probably wouldn't work out because of our combined anxiety.

'There have been more unlikely relationships than two people with anxiety,' she says.

In response to my facial expression, Patrice says, 'You have a face that's hard to read – some would call it "resting bitch face" – you should practise smiling in the mirror.'

After the appointment I feel upset. At the next session I tell her: 'I'm thinking of making our appointments once every three months, instead of fortnightly.'

'That's ridiculous, Anna.'

She convinces me that seeing her is a safeguard against getting sick again. So I continue to stay with her.

Four days before my first-ever date, I begin to get nervous. My attempts at dating haven't begun until nine months after I realised I was bi. I pace the house.

On the morning of my date, I wonder if I've gone a bit overboard with my outfit – I'd decided to wear a flowy gown. I'm forty minutes early and I'm waiting on a patch of grass in the shade of the ferris wheel, near the magenta bougainvillea at South Bank. I wave when I see Oli walking towards me. He's right on time and I'm relieved he's shown up. He does a comical double take at my dress, lowering his sunglasses briefly. He gives me a hug and then we look at the exhibition.

After, we walk under the leafy Arbour to a chocolate café, and he orders us both lemon mint granitas. He offers to pay me for the copy of my book, but I say no, it's a gift. We walk along the river, through the communal herb garden, and I tell him I used to have my lunch in this place when I was a photography student. I show Oli a shortcut through the rainforest walk to the Nepalese temple – the Peace Pagoda that remains from World Expo 88. His hand brushes mine briefly but I can't tell if it's an accident or not as he steps sideways to let tourists pass. Walking along the river with Oli feels like the world has opened to let us in, gifting us our own dance floor with sparkling possibilities. My art and writing have been my passions for as long as I can remember and as much as I find my self through these forms, I also want to find connections with people. I want to fall in love.

After \ Trip stitch / 2019

I wait for Oli to text me about our next date. A couple of days pass, and I'm worried I've scared him away. I consult Mum. She tells me, 'If he's the right person then nothing you do will scare him away.' When I am invited to speak on a poetry panel in Geelong for the Word for Word Non-Fiction Festival, I ask Mum along. I still haven't heard back from Oli and the trip will be a good distraction from all the uncertainty about whether he is interested in a relationship or not. I've never been on a mother-daughter trip before. Though we are flying to Melbourne Airport, we have decided to go straight to Geelong and not detour. We want this to be a fun trip and not one filled with the psychological thrillers that Melbourne might bring for me.

Mum and I arrive in Geelong and find a bakery with rosewater meringues. She breaks her FODMAP diet to taste my serve of panettone bread and butter pudding. We make snack packs out of almonds and cranberries from a convenience store. I am too caffeinated with tea to sleep. Mum snores. On the third night I finally get to sleep before she does. In the morning she looks at me triumphantly.

'You snore too,' she says.

I feel nervous about my panel and can't eat anything at lunchtime. I get Mum a pass into the writers' green room and we both head in. Speaking with the wonderful and kind Andy Jackson, who is the other poet on my panel, gives me energy. We are ushered downstairs, and the audience is let in. Mum sits proudly in the front row. Despite my nerves, I know this topic well – my poems are from my life. I speak more coherently and clearly than I ever thought I could. Afterwards Mum gives me a hug and says it's the highlight of her trip. We walk to the signing table, and in the moment before people start to arrive, Andy asks me how it feels to have launched my first collection. He acknowledges it can be a strange time. I say my antidepressant dosage was increased and he nods. I know this isn't the end of my answer though. What I really want to say, as the audience arrives to get books signed, is that poetry is how I knit myself together. Having my work published for others to read and connect with is how I feel my experience is seen and heard. Poetry found me and I have kept it close. That's how it really feels to have launched my collection.

Two weeks on from my Geelong adventure with Mum, to my surprise I get a text from Oli. We decide to meet at GOMA this time. We sit in the dark in one of the video rooms where colours dance across the walls. We are the only ones in the darkened room, but he doesn't move closer to me. Outside, at the State Library café, he orders a pot of peppermint tea for us both. I manage to spill half the contents over the table, so Oli makes sure to pour my second cup for me. But it just doesn't feel like a date this time.

I can't tell if he's interested or if his anxiety is getting in the way. I mope around the house, thinking it was never going to work from the start. I don't hear from Oli all week, then all month. But when I'm invited to speak at Melbourne Jewish Book Week in May, my spirits rise again. I refuse to see May as another omen; the month I went mad exactly eight years ago. Travelling to Caulfield will be my chance to rewrite my story with better memories and I'll hopefully prove to myself that independence and travel won't always lead to madness and the need to retreat home. This time I feel ready to go back.

I tell Patrice that I'm planning to visit Melbourne in May 2020 next year for Jewish Book Week. I ask her about the risks of visiting Caulfield on my trip, with my eyes trained on her toenails. I have never been able to look medical professionals in the eyes with ease. She asks me why I want to go to Caulfield specifically, and I'm taken aback that she doesn't know this important detail about my history, even though I've been seeing her for seven years now. I explain that Caulfield was the suburb I lived in for nearly two months in 2011, right before the threads unstitched. Patrice says I should be cautious and prepared if I travel there. If my heart starts racing, I am to remain calm. I write a question in my notebook, so I don't forget.

'How about you put away your notebook?'

'I have questions I'd like to cover,' I say.

'Why don't you put it away? I ask my other patients to put their notebooks away but have never done this with you.'

'Why not?'

'I feel you have a low level of tolerability.'

'What would we do if I didn't ask the questions I needed to?'

'I don't know. Maybe we would talk more freely.'

'No thanks. I think in this session I really need to have a plan for what might work for me in an emergency when I travel to Melbourne again.'

I am thinking about what might happen if I have a panic attack while travelling. Or maybe even psychosis.

'There's Valium, and I would normally never hesitate to prescribe it with my other patients, but with you—'

'Why do you treat me differently?'

Patrice doesn't answer and lets the silence drag on. I look down at the next note on my list, my eyesight blurring with tears I don't want Patrice to see. I have written the words *starting a PhD*. A PhD is something I've never thought I'd be able to do but have begun to feel this might be a possibility, with the encouragement of my family. So I begin to talk about my exciting PhD plan to dispel the charged atmosphere. But Patrice says: 'Are you sure you want to do a PhD? I don't think that's a good idea. My other patients doing PhDs are all in hospital.'

I leave the session determined to do my PhD.

Mum suggests a girls' day out and we catch the bus to Indooroopilly Shopping Centre to have Devonshire tea. We sit in stripy booth seats in the Fleet Street section of the Pig 'n' Whistle. Vases of flowers brighten the table; paintings colour walls and lush plants press against the window to disguise the bustle of the shopping centre. It's as if we are in our own private tearoom. I tell Mum my concerns about going back to Melbourne, staring at the debris in the bottom of my teacup where bits of lemongrass and ginger try to tell me my future. I cannot decipher their pattern.

'Will you come with me when I visit Caulfield?'

Melbourne Jewish Book Week is more than six months away, but I want to know if Mum is keen to go with me on a trip again. I expect to feel surreal in the environment. I can already feel parallel timelines opening as my selves collide and pass each other like ghosts. I want to take my woodcutter-mum to help battle the wolf. Sure, Caulfield might be wonderful as I show Mum Glick's bakery and the Judaica book shop, but I want someone as a companion, someone to ground me – just in case. I don't know what memories Caulfield will bring, or what dangers could reawaken the psychosis beast. But Mum says she'd love to come with me, and we start to get excited about the trip. A couple of months later, the first case of COVID-19 is detected in Australia.

After \ Unpick / 2020

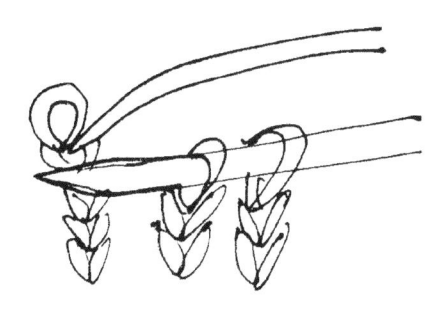

The pandemic hits. I contact my friends by email, checking how they are. My friend Anne is worried her wedding might be cancelled. Charlotte and I are bridesmaids. Anne's fiancé is French, and his family might not be able to make it to Australia due to potential travel bans. I haven't been able to sleep properly for the past two nights and haven't left the house. I fill out an online shopping order for a supermarket delivery for the family. Pasta, rice, tissues, and antibacterial wipes are limited to two packets per person. Most of the delivery timeslots are booked out, but I score one for three days' time. When we get takeaway pizza for dinner, Dad asks me if I've seen matzah in stock while online shopping. I say I haven't looked – Passover is in three weeks, and I say I doubt we'll be able to celebrate it all together with the extended family. Mum, Dad, and Alan shout out in protest.

Melbourne Jewish Book Week is cancelled along with my chance to travel with Mum to Caulfield. My synagogue closes for the first time in its 134-year history. Online articles have appeared on how to deal with COVID-19 anxiety. One article says that journalling is important during these times and historians are recommending this too. Not only can writing be a kind of therapy but documenting memory during the pandemic is important from people of all perspectives and countries. I reach for my pen to keep a dream diary. I keep multiple diaries. Writing helps give me a sense of purpose; a feeling of control, to document my life. We are still going to celebrate Passover at home, just the four of us. My room begins to look more erratic; clothes and books are everywhere. The earlier tidying is completely undone – an echo of my state of mind.

My current medication regime has become ridiculously fatiguing and isn't helping my depression or anxiety, so Patrice has suggested I see another psychiatrist, Dr Brett, for a second opinion.

'Sometimes I don't know what to do with you,' she says.

Four years ago, I insisted on coming off my antidepressant with Patrice's 'help'. But I now know the tapering schedule she prescribed me had been too fast. I feel the debilitating and disruptive side effects I experienced were not my 'underlying condition' returning, as Patrice believed, but the withdrawal effects from coming off an antidepressant too quickly. I had reached the lowest dose after many gruelling months, but she persuaded me to go back on the antidepressant at an even higher dose than I'd been on with James. I had taken one step forward, ten steps back.

On my way to the second opinion my thoughts whirl about how I finally disentangled myself from Centrelink the previous year, which had made me ill with its inhumane requirements and protocols. I even needed Dad, who fortunately looks like Robert De Niro in a mafia role, as a support person at one of my Centrelink provider appointments. I'd lost a 'secure' job three months in because I couldn't work multiple days in a row at that time due to the sedating effects of my medication at the higher dose I'd been prescribed. The workplace managers, while touting their inclusivity as an equal opportunity employer, had quickly bullied me out of my job when I disclosed my disability and my requested workplace adjustments. I now try to centre myself as I walk into the waiting room. Dr Brett's office has plush green carpet. Like in my appointments with Patrice, I look at the floor – the carpet is calming – I am nervous about getting a second opinion.

'What's your PhD on, if you don't mind me asking?'

I'd started my PhD in creative writing just before the pandemic was declared. I am lucky to have Kári as my PhD supervisor, who treats me with respect and is excited by my creative challenge of writing a memoir with so many missing memory gaps.

I tell Dr Brett a little about my project so far; that the narrative I write as the creative practice component of the PhD, my memoir, allows me to take back agency and control of the story that nurses wrote in my hospital file. I started by researching Narrative Medicine, a field which can create conditions for empathy between doctor and patient through storytelling. I wanted to shift the focus to the patient rather than the viewpoint of those in power – the medical practitioner – as a key part of my research, and highlight the imbalances that exist. I've also recently discovered the works of activists and researchers in the field of Mad Studies – a field that I hadn't known existed, which draws on the lived experience of those who identify as psychiatric survivors and other facets of being a mental health patient to create new futures for mental health knowledge. I am mainly looking at how psychiatric survivor storytelling through cross-arts forms like braided memoir, electronic literature, and Graphic Medicine such as comics and art can provide methods to create more varied and diverse in-depth representations of lived experience. I tell Dr Brett I am also writing about and researching memory and selves. He interrupts my spiel.

'Retrospective falsification,' he says.

'Pardon?'

'It means cognitive distortion. Memory is altered and is usually consistent with one's emotional state. I see this in patients every day. For example, when you're happy you can't remember when you're depressed as easily. But when you're depressed, you reframe how you see things and remember only the bad times. When we construct memory, this is also influenced by our mood. It sounds like a really interesting project.'

I'd read that the 'return to place' can trigger memories of that place and that this was also true for emotional states. Talking with a doctor who seeks to encourage and extend, however small, is such a difference from Patrice, who has never heard of Narrative Medicine or Mad Studies. Early on in my research, I'd come across the social model of disability. Unlike the medical model, that insists people are disabled by their own differences, the social model demonstrates how it is society and its systems that disable and limit a person through barriers, attitudes, exclusion, and inequality. This concept shift had changed how I viewed myself, in a positive way. Dr Brett asks me to come back for a follow-up appointment the next week. I still don't know what new medication regime he'll suggest as part of his second opinion, or if the clinic will close due to COVID-19. He asks me to email him a list of my past medications and their side effects and benefits, from what I can remember. He also asks me to fill out a Mood Assessment Program (MAP) survey from the Black Dog Institute. I throw in PDFs of my hospital file, tribunal report, and Involuntary Treatment Order from 2011.

The second session takes place a week later via phone, as the clinic is closed to patients as a safety measure. I'd expected more questions at my second session, but Dr Brett already has thoughts he wants to share. I'm sitting in my study, phone cradled in one hand and my other hand skating paper with pen. On the front door to my study, I've blu-tacked a DO NOT DISTURB sign. What Dr Brett is saying is about to change everything. He sounds like a detective; his voice is restrained and reassuring, but there's a level of excitement under the calm, as he reveals his findings. He says that what I experienced in 2011 sounds like a cycloid psychosis – a sudden acute onset with no clear reason, but possibly a result of me being stressed from living in Melbourne.

'Isn't that a bit worrying my psychosis was caused by stress? I get stressed all the time,' I say.

'But you haven't experienced another psychosis since then – it means you're resilient. Purely stress-driven psychosis is a better prognosis than bipolar disorder or schizophrenia.'

Was he saying what I thought he was saying?

'It sounds like you were more paranoid and bizarre than manic, from the reports in your Involuntary Treatment Order in 2011. It's not schizophrenia – you haven't had another psychosis in nearly ten years now, and your MAP results suggest you are unipolar.'

If I did not have bipolar disorder as my diagnosis, as I had been told for the past nine years, then what did I have?

'You have multiple anxieties. The anxiety is the primary concern. The major depressive episodes come on top of that.'

'So that means—'

'Your mood is secondary to your anxiety and phobias,' Dr Brett explains. 'Your anxiety is unrelenting and pushes your mood down. Because of your anxiety, your mood is low. Because your mood is low, you get anxious.'

My menstrual cycle has also always plagued me. Weeks before menstruation, my mood sometimes plummets so far that I need to schedule events around these weeks so that I don't burst into tears when I don't want to. When I had once asked my endocrinologist if my menstrual cycle was a factor in my psychosis in 2011, he said it would have been a probable contribution. I bought a ring: a silver crescent with labradorite full moon. A stone that holds strong through change and gives strength and perseverance with its lilac sheen. Balances and protects. I research how the Jewish calendar follows the lunar cycle and type in dates to track the moon's movements the week I went mad in 2011. A total eclipse had taken place during the week leading to my madness. According to Jewish sages an eclipse is an omen and indication of a hard time ahead. My mind had unravelled as the blood moon soared high above the hawthorn tree outside my family home.

Dr Brett suggests I try a different antidepressant and trial decreasing my antipsychotic medication dose, which has not been adjusted since nearly a decade ago when I'd been discharged from hospital. After he ends the phone appointment, I sit at my desk for a few moments. I type up my scrawled notes. I do not have bipolar disorder, I say to myself, as my brain rewires its thought processes. I do not have bipolar disorder, I say to myself, as the new world becomes even stranger. I peel off my bipolar diagnosis and wrestle it to the floor. Let its knitted shape lie still, then watch it vanish – first the knots, then the lumpy pompoms. I grieve for my diagnosis of nine years. Perhaps my old diagnosis is still lurking, waiting, tricking the doctor and me. But what even is a diagnosis but an attempt to box and label?

Patrice disagrees with the second opinion and believes I still have a mood disorder. While she says I can try cross-tapering to the different antidepressant when I'm ready, she makes no attempt to decrease my antipsychotic dose, which is not only sedating, and negatively affecting my physical health, but mind-fogging – sometimes my thoughts are like fish in a stream that keep swimming past. I am unable to grasp them unless I write them to the page when they flick their tails. The toing-and-froing with my diagnosis is enough to make me decide labels aren't so helpful. I never want psychosis to happen again. But there's something more to this thought – it's the mental health system and hospitalisation that I am more wary and fearful of. Society's dangerous mental health care system took my agency. I will always be on the lookout for the psychosis and memory loss that split my self because of what this led to – losing my rights in hospital. At home, everyone is getting used to my changed diagnosis, including me. Mum gives me fig and rose soap and says, 'here's to new beginnings.'

I'm in charge of the Seder plate for my family's first pandemic Passover without the extended family.

'We're having an orange on it,' I say.

I'd first discovered the addition of an orange in the *Guidebook to Queer Jewish Spirituality* – that an orange is added to the Seder plate to be inclusive of marginalised identities within Judaism, including women and queer people, and honours what these communities bring to Jewish life. Luckily, we have a bag of oranges. We set up in the dining room where the dark redwood dresser from my maternal great grandma sits. I love the compartment on its left-hand side that holds the challah covers and waxy Shabbat candles. The scent on opening the drawer is steeped in ritual.

I make matzah balls. As I mix the matzo meal, vegetable oil, ginger, pepper and salt, and almond meal with boiling water, Mum tells me a story. That when her Nana B – my great grandmother – escaped on the ship from Poland when she was in her twenties, she remembered all the family recipes; nothing was written down. When asked how to make a recipe and what quantities to use, she would always reply in Yiddish: 'a bisl, a bisl', *a bit, a bit*. Recipes were passed on through osmosis, through watching, and through taste. When my nana realised she wouldn't be able to use her hands for much longer from worsening multiple sclerosis at the age of sixty, she handwrote her mother's recipes in a book called *Grandmother Remembers – Family Recipes*. Each recipe has the Jewish holiday above it. The Passover matzah ball recipe is edged with autumn leaves, the colour of strawberry and apricot jam from a Purim Hamantaschen. Mum has set up the bench with all the ingredients, paper towels, and a mixing bowl, like a proper cooking school class. She remembers taste-testing the matzah ball mixture at every stage with her mother and when she tastes my mixture, she says 'tastes like Passover', and proceeds to add lashings of ginger, salt, and pepper at triple the quantities. We taste it again – much better.

We don't have a traditional Seder plate, so I choose metal bowls we usually save for Rosh Hashanah dessert. In place of a lamb shank bone, I use a boiled chicken leg from the chicken soup and roast it under the grill. For the maror I use horseradish and another dish of onion and lettuce. I make the charoset and add curly parsley to the next bowl. The last bowl will contain the roasted egg, the festival sacrifice. Before adding it to the Seder plate, I place the egg in a clay bowl and hold a match to the eggshell, until one side turns golden. Yesterday I'd baked a flourless apple, almond and ginger cake for the Seder dessert. It turned out browned and flat – perfect for Passover, where nothing must rise.

Of all the Jewish festivals, Passover is my favourite. I remember stories of Seders going until 2 o'clock in the morning. My uncle is the most practised in running the Seder in Hebrew. COVID-19 is separating us from our extended family this year, and this is unusual for us all.

This year with Mum, Dad, and Alan, we muddle our way through as best we can. We each have different Haggadah editions – the text read at the Seder, which is like trying to follow several different versions of the same story, each vying for their own particular phrasing. Dad's and Mum's Haggadahs had been given to them for their Bar and Bat Mitzvah. Mum's Haggadah still has her inscription in it, with intricate coloured illustration plates. Dad's is ornate leather, with a copper square engraved on the cover of the wavy-lined Mediterranean Sea. Alan's has golden letters embossed on the front cover, and mine is the children's Haggadah, with scenes created from plasticine from the claymation *The Animated Haggadah*. I treasure my Haggadah, including the wine stains and matzah crumbs wedged in its spine from three decades' worth of Passovers.

There's something comforting and familiar about the traditions and order to the night. For as long as I can remember, we have eaten the same dishes once a year on the night of the full moon: boiled egg chopped up in salt water – tears of the slaves, gefilte fish with a boiled carrot and red chrain (horseradish) on top, my mother's famous matzah ball chicken soup, the main meal (tonight Dad has made a curry), then Passover cake, almonds, and dark bitter chocolate. The following eight days are also filled with symbolism – no bread, or pasta, or anything that rises – the slaves escaped Egypt in such a hurry, their dough didn't have time to rise. The Passover festival is one of liberation.

As I stand over the freshly made Seder plate to photograph it, I can smell its magic – the raw onion mingling with the lettuce and scent of horseradish, the flame from the roasted egg, the sweet charoset and its grated red apple mixed with walnut meal and wine, the earthy scent of the chicken leg. This is the first time I've brought out my digital SLR for my own art project in ages. I go into photography mode as Mum sets the table. I stand on a chair for an aerial view of the table and Seder plate, and then take photographs from every other angle. I've become so invested in photographing the table, it has taken on a different meaning for me: I am the preserver of this moment in time. While the world is falling apart, this one thing, Passover, will remain the same. I put plastic wrap over the Seder plate, ready for sunset. The table is set, and I have photographed and documented every inch of it. The stage is ready.

In the kitchen, I chop the egg with a knife and pour the salt water. We eat the egg with silver teaspoons, unwrapped from their earlier cellophane. The cutlery set was a gift from Nana and Grandad, for my parents' wedding. Next, I scoop the gefilte fish and place a piece of orange carrot on top. The bottle of red horseradish is passed from person to person.

A matzah dumpling in a silky bowl of soup follows. The matzah ball is light and fluffy, ginger spiced. When it's time to find the afikomen, the middle piece of matzah that Dad has hidden, we go searching. I discover it wrapped in a blue serviette on the piano.

'The rituals seem even more meaningful in a pandemic, more magnified,' says Mum.

The Passover Seder has anchored her – stopped her from being at sea. She says she noticed how it has anchored me too – how I've rushed around preparing the eggs and gefilte fish, fully absorbed in the ritual of the familiar. The timing of Passover in the first few months of the pandemic has stopped us from being tossed about in an unpredictable ocean of fear. The rituals have held us steady and together.

After the eight days of Passover, when I see Dad in the kitchen the next morning, I'm surprised to see him with a cake tin.

'I'm making polenta corn bread,' he says.

The following day, Dad bakes Irish soda bread; the next day, Greek cornbread with feta and thyme. Baking and the pandemic seem to go together, especially after the carb withdrawals from Passover.

Sitting and writing helps stop my thoughts from circling my head. Helps me work things out. I start to think that maybe my story doesn't have to end with a trip to Melbourne, which won't be reopening its borders anytime soon. As Victoria has a second wave of COVID-19, maybe my story, this chapter of my life, will continue in Brisbane. I feel disappointed my curiosity won't be sated about what memories Caulfield may or may not bring, but also relieved. Yes, I might have been able to create positive memories to replace the older ones around the uneasy unravelling. Yes, I might have been able to lessen the tight weave Melbourne has on my consciousness. But maybe I also need to focus on creating new memories for myself here, in Brisbane, not reawaken old ones in a city I once lived in for seven weeks. It's okay if I don't go back now.

Giving myself permission not to rush to Melbourne, especially during the pandemic, is a reprieve. Besides, I want to explore different experiences that aren't wrapped up in that time of unwellness; that wintery time, filled with oblique icy rain, when I'd tried so hard to connect with my culture. That my unravelling occurred in Melbourne, the first time I'd tried to be independent, had taken away my confidence in myself. I occasionally wonder if the stress of moving to a new city had hurried the psychosis along, or if it would have torn its way out of me eventually no matter what. I imagine the madness now lying dormant, ready to erupt into a second episode when I am next unwell, perhaps only because of the narrative that Patrice and others in the mental health care system have told me. The constant pressures and fears are holding me back – I am looking over my shoulder for something I cannot see. I need to regain my independence. It's time for me to leave my family home again – besides, my poetry friends still have a spare room available.

Despite my fear that living away from home might lead to my unravelling again, I am moving out. My friend Anne, along with Alan and Dad, helps me make the move out of home. We load everything into the boots of both cars. It's the first time I've seen Anne in person since the pandemic started. We talk about her wedding, which had to be postponed in May. But Anne is down to earth about it. They help me unload my bags and suitcases. Later, I mix flour and oats in a red bowl. I bake Dad's soda bread recipe in the oven and eat it with butter and feta. I am regaining my independence. Fitting back into the fabric of the sharehouse. This time will be different, I tell myself.

I can't watch movies depicting people hooked up to memory-erasing machines like in *Eternal Sunshine of the Spotless Mind*. I can't even watch *Finding Dory*, the sequel to *Finding Nemo*, a children's animation about a blue and yellow freckled fish with short-term memory loss. For me, the aftermath of ECT meant that for months I had to record the day in my diary and rely on my mother's patience in answering questions I had asked the previous day. I cannot watch *50 First Dates* again. I also can't watch the news ever since a segment appeared on *The Project* one night on ECT. I took one look at the mouthguard placed into the patient's mouth and the gel rubbed on either side of their forehead where the electrodes would connect and rushed away from the television. I have no memory of a mouthguard being placed in my mouth. Perhaps they only do this after the anaesthetic hits. That these details aren't in my knowledge or memory is because I did not get a say.

How quickly control and agency can be whisked from underneath like a woven rug that has been covering the Kraken's sea-monster eyes. In 2011 I was pulled into ocean depths, wrestling with this colossal squid-like legend, my own threads ripped as easily as strands of hair. When I woke – as though from a coma, with no memory of the events – I had travelled so far away from myself. The Trauma-Kraken cracked a hole in the universe with a single tentacle. The sea-monster left me with stray stitches to bind together, while taking away my memory of how to tie knots. It is only by rereading my diaries and finding the writing I kept, that I can piece my story together from that first time of madness. While the madness split my self, it's the mental health system, being hospitalised, enforced ECT and psychiatric medication with damaging side effects, and the taking away of my agency by medical professionals, that form some of my greatest traumas. I fear for my future that it could happen all again.

For some people, ECT is lifesaving, and they choose to have the treatment. Families of involuntary patients do not get a choice in the treatments given, but my parents witnessed that ECT did get me out of the psychosis. This is how they felt they got me home. Despite this, I am still angry about being given ECT without my consent. As an involuntary patient, I experienced a violation of my human rights and this act can reverberate with its own trauma, causing more harm than good. It is documented that more women than men receive ECT. Gender bias still exists in health care and research, as it has throughout history.

After \ Unravel / 2020

Towards the second half of the year and end of 2020, all the progress I made with being independent begins to unravel. It's as though my antidepressant has turned on me, especially when Patrice pushed the dose higher again. I can't sleep. I cry and can't stop. At the bus station I wear my sunglasses so no one can see me. I hold onto the bench, worried that I will accidentally propel myself in front of the oncoming traffic. Perhaps it's because I'm on my way to yet another psychology appointment. Patrice has told me that Dolores is a senior psychologist and that I should see her. My first appointment with her is the day before I come out publicly on Bi Visibility Day. Waiting months for the appointment has been difficult and sometimes I feel like I am only just hanging on. I am wary about the appointment, but my hopes rise when Dolores asks me what methods don't work for me. I tell her I don't like cold psychology theories drawn out as inaccessible graphs that don't connect with me. She asks, 'when did your anxiety start?'

'As a six-year-old. I had a dream about a fox.'

'What was the fox doing?'

'It was trying to attack me, and when I woke up, the shadow of the fox's ears was on my wall. I thought it had come out of my dream into the waking world.'

Dolores laughs at this.

'Yes, things aren't what they seem,' she says.

'I screamed so loud the windows shook. For the next four years I slept on the floor of my parents' room. I was taken to a woman who my parents called the "sleep lady". Later I realised she was a child psychologist.'

I tell Dolores how after many appointments the child psychologist got fed up, lost her cool and hissed at me: 'You are making your parents tired and sick with your antics.'

But I understood that the force of my night fears was beyond my control.

'Please tell me this is the worst experience you've had with psychologists.'

'No—'

I think of the counsellor I'd seen during my Honours year, who'd rubbed my knees because he said he wasn't allowed to hug his clients.

'What helped you stop sleeping on the floor when you were a child?' she says, without waiting for me to elaborate.

'I stopped when my parents went out and a babysitter stayed one night. She told me there were dust mites in the floor that would make my asthma worse. Her staying the night broke the cycle. That's why I've never wanted theories or modules or diagrams in psychology. I just want someone to talk to, who can listen and give me their thoughts back in a down-to-earth and accessible way. Practical – you know?'

I start to tell Dolores I am coming out publicly on Instagram tomorrow.

'Have you told your family, your friends?'

She says this in an accusing tone that makes me pause. Perhaps Patrice has recommended yet another dud.

'Yes, I have told them actually.'

My rainbow poetry friends all gave me support when I reached out and asked for their advice about coming out. But I have still been trying to work up the courage to let my oldest friends know this extra part of my identity. I sent them a poem I'd written about it, and one by one they each replied in a positive way. I was relieved; through the act of telling them I am lighter, more myself. Dolores wishes me good luck for my Instagram post tomorrow and I realise the hour is up.

'An hour is never long enough,' she says.

Even though Dolores speaks over the top of me with haphazard guesses at what she thinks I am going to say, I desperately want to connect – I have waited so long to see her and don't want the disappointment of her not being the right fit for me. I have never found a psychologist I connect with. Each previous encounter makes me more resistant to trying again. I push my concerns about Dolores to the side.

The next day I get a text from Mum wishing me a very happy day and that September is such a beautiful month of renewal and beginnings. It feels like my birthday. It's just a matter of what time I'll make the Instagram post to the world saying, 'Happy Bi Visibility Day'. I finally get up the courage at 10am. The love hearts start pouring in as soon as I post. The same number of people who have liked my other Instagram posts in the past send love hearts. The support gives me courage, and I feel proud. Then the day ends, and life continues.

I hit more roadblocks in my psychology sessions with Dolores. All my worries and neuroses are scratched up like a scrub turkey digging around. I am unsettled and emotionally drained after each appointment. After my third session I start to despair – Dolores won't be able to help me after all. I ruminate over exercises I can't connect with, feeling the ones she's chosen don't respect the difficulties I have with anxiety in the first place.

But when the receptionist says Dolores is suddenly booked up until April next year, and I only have bookings until December, I hear myself sobbing in the waiting room. I have already waited so long to see Dolores this year and the more my thought processes are exposed, the less control and agency I feel I have over these new ways of thinking. Being told that there is a four-month wait and left in the lurch with my anxieties freshly turned over seems cruel to me. Dolores doesn't come out of her room to check on me, even though surely everyone in the office can hear my distress. Perhaps I won't continue with her after December – I have told Dolores I don't like graphs, models, and cold theories, but she persists in spending entire sessions on cognitive models and diagrams of generalised anxiety disorder. I don't want flow charts and inaccessible theories. I want Dolores to listen to me.

I can't sleep and this brings back the old fear. Lack of sleep for me is a sign that things are not going well. Would psychosis erupt again as it had all those years ago? I can't sleep for the second night in a row. I try to distract myself but all I can think of is that not sleeping is the first sign of being unwell, which could lead to psychosis. Everything seems to lead back to my madness. The fact that I don't want the psychosis to happen again, and don't want to lose control and agency again, is fuelling my anxiety.

I know the importance of exercise for my mental health. Each time I walk to get my groceries, I pass the ballet school. I discover it has adult beginner classes and I decide to give it a try. When I turn up to my first class on Saturday morning, the receptionist, who I discover is also a ballet dancer, greets me. On the floor are jam drops and plush bunnies. The children's class is just finishing, and lunch boxes and toys await in designated squares on the floor. In the adults' class, I am welcomed by a fellow dancer, who wears the most glorious outfit. Russet leotard with a floaty skirt; her hair is always coiffured, make-up impeccable. Our teacher doesn't judge us, isn't strict and lets us muddle along until we feel comfortable. She uses metaphors she's made up to help us picture the movements, like carrying heavy water bottles in our hands to make us do fuller, sweeping movements, to having our eyes linked to our hands with invisible strings. As we do our plies at the bar in front of mirrored studio walls, she asks us to zip up our legs like snap-lock bags.

'Does that feel different?' she asks us with each suggestion.

Soon I begin going to ballet twice a week. For the first few sessions I wear socks, and then I order a pair of my very own ballet flats online. It's still the pandemic, and there's no way I'm going to the city yet, so I hope for the best with sizing. When they arrive, I touch the pale pink ballet flats and pull them on. They fit perfectly. Now I can see how my feet point and arch and it makes being a dancer feel more real.

'Will we be able to see you dance in the end of year concert?' ask Mum and Dad when I tell them I've started ballet.

'I don't think they do concerts for the adult class,' I say.

But at the next class, our teacher comes in to tell us exciting news – they are opening up dancing roles to the adult class for the end-of-year production. We will be wearing long ornate dresses and acting on the edges of the stage. I am so excited I can hardly follow the steps for the rest of the class. It's an extra hour rehearsal;

we'll be given simple patterned stepping routines, and be paid a concert fee. I think of my performance anxiety but remind myself that with ballet, it's something new and different, and this feels freeing. There are no expectations, I tell myself.

I send Dolores a long email asking her plans for our next ten sessions. The following day, she calls three times while I am out, and I call her back as soon as I get home. She sounds distracted and I hear cars whipping past.

'Look, I don't think we are the right fit, but come in for another appointment and we can talk about it, okay?'

Trying to fix the therapeutic relationship with Dolores is the last thing I want to spend my time doing.

'I don't want t—'

'I'm actually sitting in my car in the driveway after a long day, Anna.'

'Oh sorry—'

I feel angry at myself for apologising. Dolores had been the one to try and contact me after all. I call reception to cancel all my future appointments with Dolores, recognising finally that her methods don't work for me, and that she doesn't listen. It's as though she is rehashing the same old lessons she has learned and isn't prepared to adapt to someone who might not benefit from the straight CBT guide. But the receptionist says to talk it over with Patrice first. I know I will feel physically sick if I am forced to see Dolores again. On the way home from my last appointment, I'd worn my sunglasses to hide my tears, but the train station staff still called out to me, asking if I was okay. They'd shown more care than Dolores ever had to me.

My negative experiences with psychologists make me wonder if I should avoid them altogether. I remember being ten: my need to make sure nothing bad will happen takes the new form of rituals I must complete. I start flicking the light switch in the bathroom, after I brush my teeth, until it feels just right, like I have made the world safe by using exactly the right amount of flicking, pressure, and rhythm of my finger against the nub of the switch. If I mess it up, then I must start again. If I do not do this, I know something terrible will happen. I keep the light-switch ritual a secret because something tells me to. I know it has gotten out of control when I can't stop the on-off flicking, the sequences becoming longer and longer. Again, I feel that something is wrong with me, that surely no one else in the world does this, and I don't know what to do to stop it.

My night-time ritual seeps out into the day. I fear being the one to turn off the lights for the projector at school. If asked, I know I'll have to flick the switch at least a few times for good measure, to keep everyone safe. Perhaps I'll be able to keep the sequence short, but maybe not, depending on how it feels. Then my secret will be out, and I'll be in trouble. I sit very still each time the projector is rolled out, eyes trained on the carpet. I know I must try and stop my light switch flicking when I see the ritual isn't protecting me. Instead, it's making me exhausted and trapped by its whims. One night, I grip one hand with the other to stop myself from touching the bathroom light switch again. I wait with my breath beating in my ears. I walk out of the bathroom without doing the ritual. The world doesn't crack open and nothing bad happens, even though I know it will eventually.

Soon I can walk past the light switch without even having to grab my hands. I realise that I can rely on myself and don't need the help of others; there is no need to ever tell anyone of my secret trouble. Grade Four becomes more bearable, and I can concentrate more on the lessons.

I hadn't needed the meddling of a psychologist back then at age ten. I had gotten through on my own. It would be good to have a genuinely kind therapist to talk with, to act as a sounding board. But maybe I've experienced too much of not being listened to. Maybe it's too much of a risk to continue the search in finding one again and again.

The GP I discover on my side of town near the share house is kind and down to earth, and I can see he cares. Such a difference from Dolores. When I get bitten by a spider in the garden, he cleans the spider bite and sends a sample away for testing. I see him again the following week for the results. The bite hasn't become infected and hadn't been venomous. Before the end of my appointment, I complete a Depression Anxiety Stress Scale (DASS) survey and he says my stress is higher this last week than my anxiety and depression, and that I can talk with him anytime.

I book in to see my GP for the third week in a row, even though my session with Patrice is only three days away. But I know Patrice won't be able to see me any earlier. I get to the GP practice an hour early because I can't deal with being in my room with my thoughts for a second longer. My GP gives me three numbers: Lifeline, Beyond Blue, and the Mental Health Unit at the public hospital. He tells me to book an appointment with him in a week's time, or earlier if I need to. It's a half-hour appointment and he bulk bills me. I decide to take his advice to go for a morning walk to get sun on my face early each day. But it's too late – the walking does not help, and I end up crying through the whole route.

I walk to an expensive café down the road. I order scrambled eggs in a quiet crying voice. I send Anne and Charlotte a text that

I might not be able to make the journey by bus to brunch the following day, and that I am going through a rough time. Anne calls and I cry again on the phone. She asks me if I want her to come over, but I say I'm at a café and going to ballet soon. Anne says that ballet will be a good distraction. The music gets louder at the café, but I can just hear her. Then a waitress asks if I can leave now, as there are people waiting for a table. I realise they have slowly been turning up the volume to try and get me to leave. I've been kicked off my table after spending $18 on scrambled eggs. I say bye to Anne on the phone. As I pass the café counter on my way out, I hear the barista say, 'we get all the rejects here' and know I am probably hearing things.

At the full ballet rehearsal, I watch the professional dance students do pointe work and afterwards, see their heels are raw and bleeding. The adult beginner class watches and waits to be called on and I feel like a fraud. My performance anxiety returns. I know I cannot do the concert. I leave rehearsals early and catch the bus to my family home. Alan is here, but Mum and Dad don't get back from their holiday up the coast until tomorrow. I have a feeling I'm not well. I have a sense that something bad is coming. I have been watching for this moment ever since that first time, wondering if it will come back. I make a list of people I need to tell while I still have this window of sanity. I email my PhD supervisors to let them know. The list grows. I haven't slept properly for the past week. I don't sleep all night again. At 5.30am I text Anne to ask if she can keep me company after she has breakfast. She texts me back, saying she is awake – that her fiancé is going surfing, and she can be here at 7am. My breathing is shallow. I have a crying anxiety attack where I can barely get my breath. I don't want ECT forced on me again, don't want to flick into psychosis. When Anne arrives, I've managed to set the table. She has brought a sample of wedding cake she is thinking of having at the reception – a lemon meringue sponge. I don't even know if I'll be able to make it to her wedding in two weeks or if I'll be in hospital.

I play a card game with Anne, listen to her reassurance, and eat trial-wedding-cake. Anne is an avid cook and baker, and she looks through all the family cookbooks, commenting on recipes that sound delicious. I feel my heart rate slow, my breathing return to normal. Charlotte joins Anne and me when she can a few hours later. I am calmed down enough by my friends' presence to feel okay about having a nap after they leave. When Mum and Dad arrive back from their holiday, they are confused. I have baked a cinnamon teacake, but they need time to adjust to the fact I am unwell. Alan goes for a swim in the pool and stays in for an hour doing laps, while I tell Mum and Dad that I may have to go to hospital again.

Dad drives me to Patrice's office. Patrice tells me I need to go into hospital to cross-taper my current antidepressant to the new one. Now. She doesn't think I have psychosis, but she says I do have acute anxiety. I'm so relieved it's not psychosis I don't react when she recoils after seeing something scuttle from across the room. I ask if there's a giant spider in the office.

'No, a cockroach, would it upset you if I kill it?'

It climbs through the files of patients in the cabinet. She squishes the roach in her fingers with a tissue. It upsets me more than I'd thought. I want to time the hospitalisation so I can make it to Anne's wedding.

'I'm a bridesmaid.'

The roach crawls from the bin to the floor with prehistoric powers. Patrice stomps on it five times.

'I think that can be arranged,' she says.

I buy my family four custard-filled doughnuts to break the news.

Mum gives me a plant cutting in a jar of water to keep in my room. Gardenias leak tears from hidden cracks. Alan drives me to the chemist. We get stuck behind a bus with a wrap-around advertisement asking: R U OK? On the radio, the lyrics 'everything's gonna be all right' play from Shawn Mullins's song 'Lullaby'. I tell my housemates I am unwell and am staying with my family until my hospital admission. I sleep for the next two days and nights at my family's home. Anne's hens' night is in a week and then I am scheduled to go to a private psychiatric hospital the day after her wedding.

I will probably spend the whole of Chanukah in hospital. Perhaps Chanukah's story of the miracle of light will be symbolic in some way. I won't be able to light a menorah with matches in my hospital room, so I decide to order an LED one. The menorah is travelling from Melbourne, and I hope it arrives in time. I start taking photos on my phone of everyday things to look at, for when I'm in hospital. Outside our house, I take photos of the coloured clay birds Mum has decorated the plant pots with. Mum has made the house quirky and beautiful with her choices in decorations and furnishings. I recall a conversation with Patrice.

'You rely on your mum a lot.'
'Only since 2011.'
'Can you remember how you managed before then?'
'I just relied on myself.'
'Do you remember how?'
'No.'

How do I rely on myself for inner strength, guidance, and support, when I am unwell in my self?

The next session with Patrice does not go well. She says not to be snippy with her and that she feels under attack. She says she can't just 'wave a magic wand' to make me feel better. I've had Patrice as my psychiatrist for nine years now. When things start spiralling with my health, the sessions turn as bitter as a dissolving antidepressant. That she can only handle me when things are smooth sailing should have alerted me that she wasn't right years ago. Why do I find it so hard to leave Patrice? Is it because I think my sanity is at stake? Is it because medication is involved, which can cause serious harm if not managed correctly? Would the next psychiatrist be even worse? The thought of her taking even more control away from me in hospital gives me a sense of foreboding. The truth is this: I fear changing medications, and believe I am going to die in hospital.

Dad drops me at the painting studio for Anne's paint-and-sip party hens' night. All conversations take place from far away outside my body. I want to paint a rainbow macaw, which worries me, seeing as I picked a macaw as my 'surprise guest' avatar in 2011, the night of my madness. I still haven't been able to crack the code for 'surprise guest' on my computer profile. But I stick with the brief – a black tree on a blue background with coloured bauble-like flowers. I turn the blue background into ocean waves.

'We've got an over-achiever here,' says the instructor looking at my canvas. 'Anna's an artist,' says Anne.

'Is Anne nervous about her wedding?' asks Dad when he picks me up.

'No – she's handling it really well.'

'If Anne isn't flustered, then you shouldn't be.'

'Very funny.'

'You need to have a plan for the wedding, so you don't get exhausted – talk with your doctor,' he says.

The wedding day will start at 8.30 in the morning with hair and make-up and will go from there until late at night.

'Patrice can't help. She'll just say she can't wave a magic wand.'

I can't sleep when I get home. I know I need to keep my hospital booking. I sob into my pillow, my crying affecting my vision so much I see flashes of light.

I join my parents on their 5.30 morning walk. I feel like a parasite, jumping from host to host. Mum reassures me that I'm not a parasite. She brings a clipping of flowers from the garden in three shades of purple and adds it to the vase in my room. The plant's name is Yesterday-Today-Tomorrow.

After \ Patterns / 2020

Dad drives and waits with me at the church for the wedding rehearsal. The priest appears in the garden and he and Dad talk as though they've known each other for years, and not seconds. Anne and her fiancé Lou arrive looking like they've just walked up from the beach: they are glowing. We run through the ceremony. Charlotte takes the lead, walking down the aisle first, for which I am grateful. Anne's nails are painted silvery blue. As Anne practises signing the registry, Charlotte asks, 'what are you going to do for Chanukah in hospital, Anna? Isn't it in a week?'

'Yeah, I bought an LED menorah. It's in my suitcase.'

'You should write a poem about that.'

After Dad and I return home from the rehearsal, Alan heats up the challah in the oven and tells me as reassurance: 'If you can read poems in front of an audience, you can hold a bunch of flowers at a wedding.' I take the biggest piece of challah.

On the morning of the wedding, my hairdresser magicks my hair into a side bun. The make-up artist uses double concealer under my eyes. I break out in a sweat; Charlotte takes one look at my sheeny face and makes us all paper fans out of blue-lined notepaper. And in no time at all, we are out of the car and walking down the aisle. My bouquet has an iris that is yet to open and falls at a right angle. At the reception we stow our bouquets in vases of water, and I get a mocktail. It's the most glamorous mocktail I've ever had, and tastes of fizzing sherbet. It feels surreal knowing what tomorrow brings: a psych ward. But tonight, I am at my best friend's wedding and Anne is a relaxed bride. In her lace white dress that clasps at her throat, she looks elegant and stunning. When Anne and Lou dance, we watch and then I join them on the balcony. Charlotte twirls me around. Mum and Dad appear, and we form a circle. By the end of the night, the iris in my bouquet has straightened and started to open and bloom. At home I unpin my hair. I remove my make-up with a washer and try not to think about tomorrow. I want to keep hold of this golden day.

Although I am going in voluntarily, I cannot write of my second hospital admission in 2020 without thinking about my first in 2011, and the hinge knitted into my selves. Unlike 2011, when I knew almost nothing of my hospitalisation at the public psychiatric hospital, I will be aware this time in the private hospital. And I plan on remembering everything, every detail – hopefully I will not even need to request my file to guess at my experience; ECT is not on the cards. I carry my bridesmaid bouquet with me in the morning to adorn my hospital room. As we enter hospital reception, the woman at the desk temperature-guns our heads.

'So, you're being admitted?' the woman asks Dad, who clearly looks more agitated than I do. Dad and I look at each other, trying not to laugh. I hug Dad goodbye. The admission process will take three hours. The nurse puts my flowers in a heavy-cut glass vase by my bedside.

'I was at a wedding yesterday. That's my bridesmaid bouquet.'

'Good Lord. And now you're here. Ever been an inpatient here before?'

'No, just an inpatient at a different hospital, ten years ago.'

I fill out forms I can't concentrate on. I answer questions like the year, the prime minister, count backwards from twenty. My nurse needs to take my urine sample but can't find the bottles. She tells me there are trays we can use in the ECT rooms. I do not want to be anywhere near the ECT rooms, especially on my first day. The rooms are cold and have a static feel. I pee in a tray, spilling half of it on my undies. I'm led to the lunchroom and eat fish with potato wedges, then chocolate cake in custard. I am exhausted and don't make eye contact with anyone. I lie on my bed in the dark for an hour and a half. My nurse tells me to download an app for my breathing. I cry while trying to be mindful.

My roommate sticks her head around the corner and says hello, waving lavender essential oils under my nose. She shows me the washing machine settings in the laundry room, the timetable for activities, the menu for lunch and dinner, and I sign up to a Pilates and yoga class with her. At night, every half an hour the torches come. I get two hours sleep. The iris in my bouquet is shrivelling up and I try not to read any signs into it. When I get called to take my photo at reception the next morning, I can only think of my mug shot ten years ago for my previous hospitalisation and burst out crying. The receptionist calls my nurse and says we can take the photo another time.

When I check my emails the next day, I read I've been awarded a scholarship for the final two years of my PhD in creative writing. I accept my scholarship by return email on my phone and ask the receptionist if she can print a copy of the forms I need to fill out.

It takes me an hour to get my head around the forms. I locate my details and instead of scanning the documents I take a photo of the papers on my phone and attach them. Mission completed. But the nurses acknowledge things will get worse before they get better as I withdraw from my antidepressant and cross-taper with the new one. My walk becomes slow and shuffling. I am slow with choosing my meal, with putting the dishes away. The yoga is too fast, and I have no strength. The textas at the craft table remind me of fragments from my first hospital admission at the public hospital. There's a sign in the kitchen hall that reads: 'Prunes May Be Contaminated' before I realise the words say: 'Prunes May Contain Seeds'.

Chanukah doesn't start until tomorrow night, but I turn on the menorah. All eight candles blaze courage and strength. Without my glasses on, the light wavers, making them look like real blue flames. I feel empowered and calm. But on the first night of Chanukah, I burst out crying in front of a small group, fifteen minutes into the 'compassion and love' guided meditation. I roll up my mat and head back to bed. I jolt upright as the emergency alarm goes off. All the nurses in the station start running. A red electronic sign illuminates the room number. I don't think I could bear it if someone took their life while I am in here. But it's a false alarm – one of the cleaners has accidentally backed into the button by mistake. The fire alarms wink at me. I remember reading in my hospital file how I'd smashed in all the alarms a decade ago.

Every nurse I've spoken to has mentioned they are glad they got out of the public system. The patients refer to the public hospital psychiatric ward as a prison and everyone feels lucky that they are in the private hospital instead. The only reason I'm able to be in the private hospital is because I now have private health insurance and am not severely psychotic. In this hospital, I can have access to my phone and devices that I can type on. I have another cup of tea. Warmth helps my hands. I wrap them around cups of peppermint. When the physio presses on points in my wrists, he says he thinks I have symptoms of carpal tunnel syndrome in both hands. He believes it's from holding my phone in bed and typing my diary and story. He tells me to rest. No drawing or writing. I email my new memoir drafts to my supervisor, Kári.

When I arrive for my night meds, I discover that Patrice has accidentally written 8am and not 8pm for my lowered dose. The nurse won't give me my meds. I don't want the withdrawal process to be any more stuffed up than it already is. I text Patrice, who confirms her mistake. I show the nurse the text, and she gives me my meds, grumbling. My hands are too sore to brush my own hair, so I email my friend Nadia, asking her for a hair-brushing session before I make the next reduction in medication. Nadia brings Chanukah doughnuts. She spends an hour brushing my hair.

'How much do you charge?' asks a girl watching Nadia brush my hair. 'Thirty years plus of friendship,' says Nadia.

Nadia has also brought me hand cream, chocolate, home-grown tomatoes from her garden, flowers, and cards. We are both wearing purple cardigans and when the hour is up, she cries when saying goodbye.

'What's wrong?'

'It's just hard leaving you in here.'

Patrice is fierce the next morning. She says I need to pick up on my own self-care and not rely on others to brush my hair. She threatens me with the public hospital if my hand doesn't improve.

'But you said I could see my friends in hospital.'

She mentions community housing. I feel as though she is physically attacking me. I should never have trusted this woman and her contradictory ways, and now I feel like I am under her control in this place. My blood pressure is the highest reading since I've been in here. I lie on my bed while the cleaners walk past me to change my roommate's sheets. There's only a thin curtain that separates us, and they talk as though I am not there.

'My husband, he has depression. I refuse to drive him places, don't want him to rely on me. He needs to get himself out of it. I'm sick of having to do everything for him.'

'Yes, we have better inner strength. We have stronger minds than these people.'

'I've heard it's going to be a full house over Christmas.'

I want to tell them that strong minds are an illusion; they have never experienced mental illness, so have no right to think they have better inner strength. I want to say that the inpatients here are more resilient than they could ever imagine. And how can they speak this way in front of me, lying in the next bed? I feel so angry at their flapping, ignorant sheet-changing shadows. I have the seven lights lit up on the menorah, even though I'm not sure what night of Chanukah it is anymore.

I sign out a snap-lock bag of washing powder to do my laundry. I sit in the laundry room listening to the washing machine. The traffic through the window makes me dizzy. The outside world is too fast. On the whiteboard are the words: *Thanks who folded my clothes / If anyone finds a grey sock, please let me know / Rules: Only use 30min cycle. Always clean lint from the dryer.*

I begin to crave popcorn. I text Anne, asking if she is free, and she brings me popcorn that she's handmade herself, along with my requested tweezers from the IGA as my monobrow is growing back. I know I'll have to ask permission from one of the nurses to cut open the sealed plastic packet of tweezers with scissors. Anne and I talk about how beautiful her wedding was and it's almost as though I'm not in hospital. I feel better today but am still hurt by Patrice's suggestion of dumping me at the public hospital and community housing. I ruminate on shards of yesterday's conversation with Patrice.

'I just want to be treated like a normal person.'

'Do you feel normal?' she counters.

This is an unfair question. Everyone deserves respect.

'I'm just being pulled every which way. I'm withdrawing from my meds to change over to the new one, you know that.'

But I may as well be talking to an empty chair. It's as though she doesn't believe in withdrawal symptoms. I see the OT to talk about sensory help for my anxiety. Afterwards, she encourages me to go on the Mount Coot-tha Botanic Gardens excursion she'll be leading at 9am tomorrow. A nice change from the hospital corridors. The OT doesn't think I'll need to go into community housing when I mention it to her. I hear my name called over the speakers that I have a delivery. The hand-brace the physio suggested I order must have arrived early. But when I get to reception, the receptionist brings out the biggest, most beautiful box of flowers I've ever seen.

'They smell really good,' she says.

'I'm going to cry,' I say, and I do, carrying the flowers proudly all the way up the corridor to my room. I open the envelope which says: 'Dear Anna, Congratulations on your scholarship. Happy Chanukah. You will feel better soon. Love Mum, Dad, and Alan.'

In the morning my family visits. We sit in the courtyard, chunks of hair floating under the table from a patient's haircut session. Seeing my family makes me more miserable – I have missed them too much. I can't even eat the biscuits Dad has especially bought from the Persian bakery at Taringa. I realise the sooner I get out of here the better. I had been led to believe that hospital was a safe place while changing medications in case I had an adverse reaction. Now I just want to get out of here. I need to go home. I have already been here for ten days. In another nine days it will be Christmas. I wait at reception for the excursion to the Mount Coot-tha Botanic Gardens. We pile into two maxi taxis. It's rained earlier in the morning, and the frogs are croaking. We see turtles and ducks paddling; a water dragon swims with his head poking out of the water. Everything feels surreal, including the brightness of the flowers after rain.

I wake the next morning feeling more clear-headed with less anxiety. I haven't died of serotonin syndrome. But I later believe the ripping-the-band-aid-off approach Patrice used with my antidepressant changeover left me with severe withdrawal effects for years. Signs are telling me it's time to leave hospital. A nurse knocks over my vase of flowers and drenches my menorah. The water pipe bursts and the whole hospital is without water or flushable toilets for two and a half hours. I text Patrice with a message that I want to go home. My departure date is moved to tomorrow. I am packed and waiting. The following hours are excruciating. I keep expecting the hospital to come down with COVID-19 just as I am about to leave, forcing me to stay here for another two weeks, imprisoned inside. Patrice gives me the worst-case scenario while she is on holiday for ten days: that I become depressed as well as suicidal, and need another admission. When the Silver Service taxi pulls up, I stare at it for a few moments, wondering if it's for me. I've been in here for two and a half weeks now. I walk to the door, open it, step out, and I am free.

After \ Woven overlay stitch / 2020–2023

'How are you?' asks my GP as we walk down the corridor to his doctor's room.

'It's good to be out.'

'You were admitted? Did you get out last week?'

'Yesterday.'

'Oh goodness. Are you staying with your family?'

'I'm back at the share house.'

He asks me what new medication I'm on, prints my scripts, and answers my questions with care. My GP tells me that I have agency for how I want my treatment plan to go, and I look at him in confusion because this is not how things have panned out for me and has not been true in my past. But just as I'm thinking how wonderful it is to have a reliable and kind GP on this side of town, he tells me he is leaving the practice for the year.

I manage to boil some vegetarian dumplings from the vegan grocery store down the street. On Christmas Day, Dad picks me up to go home for lunch and drops over some lamb curry and things for the pantry that Mum has organised: packets of rice, a banana, cans of tuna, a lemon, tomatoes, and cheese. My writing mentor Felicity, who has always supported me through difficult times for many years, has sent me flowers and chocolate and I have new poems to show her for my *Anxious in a Sweet Store* poetry manuscript, including a poem called 'Pissing in the ECT Rooms at the End of 2020'. Dad oven-bakes chickpeas that taste like popcorn. I try to make the dressing for the potato salad, but my mind can't concentrate on the recipe – the words *parsley*, *lemon juice*, and *oil* muddle in my head. I try not to feel like a failure. One of the classes in hospital was about negative thinking and the psychologist had told us not to feel like failures. I feel even more like a failure for thinking I'm a failure. Mum says to focus on the necessities: to make sure I get my groceries, and to eat and drink water regularly. To leave my room. That it will help to practise doing these things. The table fills with potato salad, green salad, and chicken. Dad bakes bread. After a break from all the food, we have a Brumby's Christmas pudding. Alan has managed to buy the last pudding in the bakery.

Nadia picks me up in the afternoon and we go back to her place for a cup of tea. When I get tired, she drives me all the way home.

'We'll be passing the hospital on the way, is that okay?'

'Yeah, thanks for the warning.'

Back at home, I eat one stick of fudge and fall asleep at 5pm, missing dinner. I manage to walk the twenty minutes to the grocery store in the morning, but it's closed for Boxing Day. I eat the Tupperware container of Dad's lamb curry. And as the days pass, I begin to get myself back. I wash my hair. I buy half a loaf of thick-cut wholemeal bread, bananas, and crunchy peanut butter. I eat, sleep, and drink water. I leave my room for walks during the day.

But as the new year rolls around, I realise the antidepressant isn't working. Patrice had continued to push the dose higher and higher before she left on holiday. Something is not right, and I know in my gut it's the new antidepressant causing me to have suicidal ideation as a side effect. Because Patrice is still on holiday, I dial the on-call psychiatrist from the hospital I've just stayed at. It's a Saturday and one of the doctors answers – but my relief quickly turns in on itself. He makes it clear he doesn't believe me that it's the meds, even though the brochure lists suicidal ideation as an adverse side effect of the antidepressant I'm taking. He says that the antidepressant I am on is generally well tolerated by his clients and he refuses to listen to my concerns. He says it's most likely related to my menstrual cycle, which I've had ongoing difficulties with, even though the weeks aren't matching up for it to be a premenstrual cause. I make an appointment to see my endocrinologist, who says it's likely my antidepressant and to speak with Patrice when she gets back.

'Do you feel you need another hospitalisation?' the endocrinologist asks.

'I don't want another one.'

At the next session, Patrice reluctantly agrees with me that I should come off the antidepressant. She mutters something about not wanting me to sue her if the next antidepressant causes even worse effects, so she asks me to choose a different drug from a stained out-of-date book that lists every antidepressant on the market. She offers no guidance and tells me to take the book home with me.

'See if you can do any better with your "choice",' she seems to say, as I look at the dizzying list of drugs and their side effects, some of which are literally listed as 'sudden death'. Later I will find the beginnings of a poem in my notes:

(un)lucky dip
you get to choose which one you try first—
the one that might kill your ovaries
or the one that might get your kidneys,
and thyroid. At least she's finally stopped
suggesting the one that starts with a rash,
and then breaks down all your organs
and you die. *I feel like all those options
are shit*, I say. *You've got bipolar,
you're already feeling shit*, she says.

I am told that going off my meds altogether is not an option, even though I've received a second opinion that I don't have bipolar. Last time I'd tried to come off the antidepressant, Patrice had believed that my underlying condition was returning rather than the side effects of withdrawal. Now I feel she is using this false belief against me again, which makes me uncertain in myself. I am free from the psychosis of 2011 but my mind and my body are still owned by doctors. My GP had said I now had a choice in my treatment plan, but I feel I don't – I am still being pushed into something I do not want because of fear. Not one doctor has ever acknowledged the harm and trauma caused by my involuntary hospitalisation and the fallout from the forced ECT treatment and continuing medication regime.

I don't pick an antidepressant from the book, and return it to Patrice two weeks after she hands it to me. She acts surprised she'd given me the book in the first place and looks at me like I am lying that she'd ever given me the choice of antidepressant. Patrice tells me again: 'I don't want a repeat of what happened at your first hospitalisation.'

'I'm on an antipsychotic,' I say, to remind her.

She talks into her water bottle – her words are muffled, and I cannot hear what she is saying.

'Your antipsychotic is already at a low dose,' she says more clearly, after removing the bottle from her lipstick mouth.

I cry with frustration, anger, and hopelessness. My dose has not been lowered since I left hospital in 2011. I am also crying with something else – grief. I am sick of her and these appointments and realise that maybe instead of fewer appointments with Patrice, I need to take a risk and change psychiatrists altogether.

'I've been on this journey with you for nine years,' she says, watching me.

No, you haven't. You may have observed me for 45 minutes once every two weeks, but you have not lived my experience, felt my emotions. To claim this is an insult.

I do not say these words, only stare at the floor, tears leaking.

'Try to stay in the present,' she says, before returning to her 'what ifs', her 'I don't have a crystal ball', her 'these are the meds we have to work with – I know they're not perfect'. She drags out silences and each time I move to speak, she cuts me off.

'What's the best thing in your life?' Patrice asks me.

'My family and friends,' I say.

'And the worst?'

I try to find the words.

'Your health,' she says, putting words in my mouth, not giving me a chance. Her eyes become even more shadowy, and she looks at me like I am dying. I know it's Patrice and the mental health 'care' system that are the worst things in my life, though I feel unsafe uttering these words in her office, so I continue to remain silent. At the end of the session, for the first time in nine years, she doesn't open the door for me, despite the session having clearly ended. Her leaving the door closed to me after nine years is the push I need to change. This final act of disrespect from Patrice flares all the inappropriate comments and upsetting remarks she's ever said to me – comments I have tried to brush away, by ignoring their barbs. Now they whiplash through my head as one. Opening the door from her office by myself is an indignity but also my freedom. Opening the door gives me the courage to leave. I let myself out and never go back.

I spend an afternoon at golden hour filming in the local park, focusing my lens on bottle brushes, jacaranda flowers, and a cat that has followed me by arching under a gap in the fence. I layer the video footage I'd taken on my 2011 Melbourne trip by dragging the clips onto the digital timeline. It's eerie watching it back – I only remember these places because they're trapped in the 2011 footage – but more than that, I start to remember filming with my small handheld camera, remember walking the corridors and travelling up and down in lifts to each level, somewhere in the city of Melbourne. I feel unsettled and exhilarated as I click 'overlay' and new juxtapositions of imagery are revealed to me.

I overlay Brisbane 2020 with Melbourne 2011. I keep the Melbourne soundtrack: my feet walking, the sound of the wind, the train, a man shovelling ice in a fish shop display. A ghostly scrub turkey walks up a Victorian staircase. A cat watches a train flicker from both sides of the fence. A clock and merry-go-round jangle among alleyways, the insides of old-fashioned elevators swing, and red and orange maple leaves are drawn into the breeze. This is the feeling I wanted from the Melbourne trip I planned to take last year. I retrace my steps digitally, through video, the sounds and images all around me. The video gives me the same uneasy sense of having been and not been there before. I do not need to go back, I tell myself. I have made my peace with this city through my video art. I call the work a collaboration between my selves. And I get my hair cut short: a transformative haircut where I will feel lighter than I have in years.

The impetus for writing this memoir was the splintering of my memory and self after psychosis in 2011. I had two selves – part one: before the madness, and part two: after the madness. The madness itself is a void that has no memory and I have had to knit and braid myself around its form. This event and psychiatric hospitalisation altered my life, my family's life, and how I saw my future. I began a process of understanding and an attempt at reclamation and agency of my experience and weaving the memories I did have around the gaps of memories I had lost. There was no one way to try this, except through knitting and assemblage, which is an ongoing exercise.

I am not casting off. I haven't researched the properties of thread; I've felt them in my hands as I've woven my tale, going by touch. My camera is still metaphorically stitched to my side and my knitting may take the human form, a scarf, a book, or something else entirely, depending on how I look at it each day. I have faith the knots and stitches and gaps I have will hold – the more holes, the more chances to work around memory. I sense the memories of these stitches will keep. Besides, I have written a record now. Part of my story from that time – creativity as survival, expression, and thriving life force.

In a couple of years, I slowly reduce the dose of my antipsychotic with a different psychiatrist, so that I am no longer as sedated. The withdrawal process is painful, both emotionally and physically, but over time I begin to get my energy back and my mood becomes less of a struggle. The knots in my body and mind that had been crochet-hooked in deep by medication's claws begin to breathe again at the lower dose: revelling in light. I will graduate from my PhD and both my external examiners will nominate me for the Outstanding Doctoral Thesis Award. People often ask me 'what's next?' and I can only reply that I will keep creating and writing. Writing and art are how I have empowered myself, on my own terms. I tell myself to remember this. After all, frayed stitches are enough to restitch with air, with words.

Acknowledgements

This book was written in Meanjin (Brisbane). I would like to acknowledge the Traditional Custodians of the land on which I live, write, work, and create – the Jagera and Turrbal people, and pay my respects to Elders past and present. As an author, I acknowledge that Aboriginal and Torres Strait Islander peoples are the land's first storytellers, and also the world's oldest storytellers. Sovereignty was never ceded.

Thank you to my mum, Sari, my dad, David, and my brother, Alan. I love you all. Thank you for reading this work in manuscript form and for providing extra notes and edits. Thank you especially to Mum for being my memory keeper, sounding board, and confidante, and for countless cups of tea. This book is dedicated to you.

Thank you to my wonderful PhD supervisors at the Queensland University of Technology: Kári Gíslason and Lesley Hawkes, for three years of support, guidance, mentorship, and insightful discussions during my PhD, which this book has grown from. This project received support through an Australian Government Research Training Program Scholarship.

I am grateful to the brilliant Felicity Plunkett for mentoring me on this project, with thanks to funds from the QUT Emerging

Writers Mentorship Prize. Felicity has helped me in more ways than I can express and her support means the world. I also received professional development funds and a mentorship with Felicity from the Queensland Premier's Young Publishers and Writers Award, which is supported by the Queensland Government through Arts Queensland and State Library of Queensland and administered by Queensland Writers Centre.

Thank you to NewSouth and to my wonderful publisher Harriet McInerney for publishing my book. I acknowledge Varuna, the National Writers' House, where I worked on the copyedits of this memoir through email correspondence with my editor, Jocelyn Hungerford. Special thanks to Maria van Neerven for her friendship and support at Varuna.

An earlier extract of my memoir won the Nillumbik Prize for Contemporary Writing (2020). Earlier versions of my memoir manuscript were also shortlisted in the Spark Prize (2020), shortlisted in the Queensland Literary Awards 'Emerging Queensland Writer Manuscript Award' (2017), and shortlisted in the Scribe Nonfiction Prize (2016). An interactive version of *How to Knit a Human* (available in the projects section on my website www.annajacobson.com.au) was shortlisted in the 2022 Woollahra Digital Literary Award – Digital Innovation Category. Earlier extracts of my memoir were published online in *Archer Magazine*, and *Jewish Women of Words*.

My visual poems about my paternal grandfather, who was a Holocaust survivor, can be read online in *Australian Book Review* 'States of Poetry QLD – Series Two'. My poem 'How to Knit a Human' was first published in *Verity La*'s 'Clozapine Clinic – the Frater Project', selected by co-editors Tim Heffernan and Alise Blayney. An excerpt from my poem 'Appointment of the Last Postman' was first published in my poetry chapbook

The Last Postman (Vagabond Press, 2018). Some of my poems from *Amnesia Findings* (UQP, 2019) and *Anxious in a Sweet Store* (Upswell, 2023) have woven their ways into my work.

Thank you to the mentors of the memoir writing workshops I attended over the years: ABC RN's Big Weekend of Books 'Q and A' Workshop with Kris Kneen; Writing the Future of Health with Andy Jackson; Red Room Poetry's 'MAD Poetry' Online Workshop series; 'Writing with Illness' with Katerina Bryant; 'Creative Memoir' with Eloise Grills; 'Write What Makes You Blush' with Lee Kofman; Kristina Olsson's QWC Memoir Workshop; Express Media's Tracks Brisbane Workshops, which included a braiding and non-traditional storytelling structure workshop with Kris Kneen; and Kate Holden's Brisbane Writers Festival Masterclass. Thank you to Katie Woods for granting me the Queensland Writers Centre Access Fund during her time as CEO to participate in 'Year of the Memoir' with Kári Gíslason in 2016.

I was inspired by Bronwyn Lea's repeated line 'they make and remake the bed' in 'Routine Love Poem' from her collection *The Other Way Out* (Giramondo, 2008). For example, I describe the beds making and unmaking themselves in the 2011 hospital scene to portray the surreal passage of time.

Thank you to Dr James Scott for his kindness and for reading my memoir in its draft form. Thank you also to my childhood GP, the lovely Dr Linda Maloney.

With thanks to my writing friends for encouraging me and having conversations with me about memory, especially Ellen van Neerven, Nathan Shepherdson, and Pascalle Burton. Special thanks to Pascalle Burton and Mirandi Riwoe, for also reading my manuscript in its draft form. Thank you to my photography friends for conversations about light, the mind, and heart. Special thanks to Peter Wilson. Thanks to my oldest friends: Anne Sawyer, Charlotte Brakenridge, Nadia Myers, Hui Li, and JR. Thank you for all the crafternoons, catch-ups, and for being here for me.

And finally, with thanks to my readers – may reading my words let you feel less alone in your experiences.

Milton Keynes UK
Ingram Content Group UK Ltd.
UKHW011042100424
440896UK00004B/23